# DEALING
## *with*
# DISAPPOINTMENT

## JOHN HINDLEY

Dealing with Disappointment *How to know joy when life doesn't feel great*
© John Hindley/The Good Book Company, 2017.

Published by
The Good Book Company
Tel (UK): 0333 123 0880
International: +44 (0) 208 942 0880
Email: info@thegoodbook.co.uk

Websites:
UK: www.thegoodbook.co.uk
North America: www.thegoodbook.com
Australia: www.thegoodbook.com.au
New Zealand: www.thegoodbook.co.nz

Unless otherwise indicated, Scripture quotations are from The Holy
Bible, New International Version, NIV Copyright © 1973, 1978, 1984,
2011 by Biblica, Inc.

ISBN: 9781784981204

Cover design by Ben Woodcraft

Printed in the UK

# CONTENTS

# 1. WE ARE DISAPPOINTED

The words of the Teacher, son of David, king of
Jerusalem:
"Meaningless! Meaningless!"
    says the Teacher.
"Utterly meaningless!
    Everything is meaningless." (Ecclesiastes 1 v 1-2)

I find this the most disturbing, the most intriguing and one of
the most attractive beginnings to any book of the Bible.

## DISTURBING

It disturbs me because it seems at odds with much of what
I think the Christian faith is—or at least should be—about.
When I think of following Christ, I picture Paul preaching in
a marketplace as the crowd grows more angry and some grow
more interested. I picture Moses walking through the wind-
held seas as the Lord himself stands behind as rearguard for
his ransomed people. I picture Abraham sacrificing a ram
instead of his son on Mount Moriah, I picture missionaries

watching the shore of their homeland slipping over the horizon, knowing they will never see it again.

When I think about following Christ, I think of a life of faith, love, hope and courage. I enjoy the truths that we can find our identity in Christ, that he gives us a commandment to love and a commission to share the good news that saved us. I often picture Russell Crowe's *Gladiator* inspiring his men by telling them that their deeds will echo in eternity. I love its half-truth: that there are deeds which echo in eternity but that they are those done in the quiet, for the least of people. I love that the smile and welcome for the refugee, the meal popped round to the sick friend and the sleep-stealing, desperate prayer that no one hears apart from the Lord of Hosts are that echo to eternity.

The Christian life is a life full of meaning, isn't it? So it is disturbing to read a Bible book that begins with a declaration of the meaninglessness of life. It is even more disturbing that these words come from the lips of the Teacher, son of David, king of God's people—from Solomon, the greatest and wisest of the kings of Israel. And it is still more disturbing to realise that these are inspired words—words inspired by the author of the Bible, David's still greater descendant, the Lord Jesus, through his Spirit. These words are just Solomon's insight, but Jesus Christ's. It is deeply disturbing to read the One who is the source of all meaning declare that life can be meaningless.

And it is even more disturbing because it is so obviously true.

## INTRIGUING

This is what intrigues me about the book of Ecclesiastes, and especially the way it begins. After his arresting start, Solomon goes on to write a tragic lament on the meaninglessness of life:

What do people gain from all their labours
    at which they toil under the sun?
Generations come and generations go,
    but the earth remains for ever.
The sun rises and the sun sets,
    and hurries back to where it rises.
The wind blows to the south
    and turns to the north;
round and round it goes,
    ever returning on its course.
All streams flow into the sea,
    yet the sea is never full.
To the place the streams come from,
    there they return again.
All things are wearisome,
    more than one can say.
The eye never has enough of seeing,
    nor the ear its fill of hearing.
What has been will be again,
    what has been done will be done again;
    there is nothing new under the sun.
Is there anything of which one can say,
    "Look! This is something new"?
It was here already, long ago;
    it was here before our time.
No one remembers the former generations,
    and even those yet to come
will not be remembered
    by those who follow them. (Ecclesiastes 1 v 3-11)

It rings so true to our day-to-day life. So much of life feels like toil. You get up scarcely believing that the alarm could possibly have the time right. The morning routine of toast, toothbrushes, lost book-bags, late buses, strong coffee (drunk cold) and screaming children, or maybe just of crushing loneliness, leaves you getting to work just on time feeling as if you've already put in a tough day. (If your morning routine consists of pootling around the house in dressing gown and slippers as your sausages sizzle in the pan and you wonder what to do on such a delightful day, then first, don't tell other people, it won't be appreciated; and second, you will come to see why this book is still for you).

After the morning of toil, there is a day of hard graft on the building site, or in the office, school, factory, home or hospital. Or worse, there is the drawn-out process of trying to fill a day that you wish contained work, but does not. The day's work might be followed by bathtimes, bedtimes, homework or emails, cooking, cleaning, bills and decisions, meetings for church, school governors, family crises or a local-issue group—or even more empty hours to fill. Sure, there is some time for relaxing with friends, family, book or screen. But the simple question, "What do people gain from all their labours at which they toil under the sun?" is intriguing. We readily accept the idea that life feels like labour and toil. We also readily acknowledge the fear that it might indeed be meaningless.

When it is Christ who declares that all things can be meaningless, then we need to sit up and listen. This is not what I expect to hear him say.

## ATTRACTIVE

Yet knowing that Jesus authored to statement that life can be meaningless—that it is no surprise to him that we are disappointed—is attractive to me. It is attractive and brings great relief. The fear that most, or all, of what we do might be meaningless is one of the hidden terrors of the Christian heart. We do not voice it often, and we hide from it even in ourselves. Most of us feel it, though. Since deciding to write this book, and talking about it with family and friends, I have been genuinely surprised by how many have said that disappointment is a serious issue for them in their Christian life—and, it seems, it is even more of an issue for my family and friends who do not follow Jesus. So I love how the real God addresses this reality. A nagging disappointment or a quiet desperation about how life has turned out might be something of a taboo subject in churches, but God sees fit to speak out on this.

The sense of meaninglessness—indeed, the reality of meaninglessness—that the Teacher of Ecclesiastes articulates is the gnawing disappointment in our souls. This disappointment is something that we feel, sometimes in a way we are only vaguely aware of, like a crocodile silently drifting below the surface, only showing nostrils and yellow eyes. Of course, like the crocodile, sometimes disappointment rears its head and sinks its teeth into us. Disappointment is a form of suffering—one of the trials of living in this broken and breaking age. It is the ongoing consequences of major suffering in our lives. For example, if your child is seriously ill or your marriage is breaking down, you will rightly feel as though you are going through a period of dark and hard suffering. Two years after the death of your child or the ending of your marriage, you will still feel the pain of it. You may also carry a burden of disappointment over what might have been, over what you have lost. There is no need to try to tease out what is suffering and what is disappointment—life is just not that simple, as you well know. But part of the pain is the sense of "what if..." and the aimlessness and emptiness of life now.

Often, disappointment is our response to the lack of something. It's why we don't tend to think of it as suffering, because we generally use that word to describe an active pain—illness, bereavement, or betrayal. But lacking something—spouse, children, friends, fulfilment—is something we all know, and it hurts. It is disappointment.

And then there is a disappointment that appears to have no root. There is nothing that we would call suffering, but also nothing lives up to what we hoped. This sense of general disappointment is what I see all around me in friends of my age—going on forty—although it is by no means limited to them. This is the sense that there is nothing obviously wrong—I have a decent job, a nice house, a good wife, healthy, growing children, and yet...

... And yet life feels empty, meaningless. In twenty years' time I will be in more or less the same job, same house, and same marriage with the same kids coming home for Christmas, (hopefully). There is nothing else to hope for beyond the Friday-night takeaway, the break over Christmas and the holiday we're planning for next summer. There are plenty of good times in life, and nothing I could really complain about. But surely there is more than this?

The strange thing about this kind of rootless disappointment is that it gets worse as you achieve your dreams. It lives at the top of the mountain that you set yourself to climb when you were young. On reaching the summit, you enjoyed the view for a while—and then you saw that there was nothing there. It was bare rock.

We don't even want to go near this sense of disappointment. We see it in the triumphant athlete who turns to drink after they retire, the multi-millionaire who is still a workaholic despite having all he could want, or the friend who retires on a good pension and goes on long-dreamed-of cruises, who sees their family regularly, and yet who finds that infirmity, illness or just the looming reality of death discolours all those perfect pictures. These figures intrigue and scare us because we want to hope that there could be more—that a lucky deal, a well-planned holiday, a child who plays professional football or who wins a Grand Slam will bring the meaning we crave. To know that the great and good struggle to find meaning is frightening.

## FINDING JOY

If you have lived, you've been disappointed. And if you've been disappointed, you've experienced the way it deadens joy and steals satisfaction. I'm guessing there are areas of quiet desperation in your life that you prefer to push to the back of your mind and try to leave there—but they keep pushing back.

What do you do with disappointment? What difference does, or can, Jesus Christ make to that disappointment? How can you be realistic about disappointments, and yet walk through life with a joy that actually grows in those disappointments?

That's what I set out to write a book about. This is it. And it's held some surprises for me. But it's definitely helped me. Jesus says life is meaningless—but that's not all he says. I don't think you'll find it easy to read this book. But I hope you'll find it liberating as it brings you face to face with the God who "in all things ... works for the good of those who love him, who have been called according to his purpose" (Romans 8 v 28).

# 2. WE SHOULD BE DISAPPOINTED

I'm surprised this chapter is here.

I had expected to write a book that would help us to turn away from putting our hope too much in the things of this world. I thought I'd be mainly writing about how we are disappointed because we expect our houses, cars, holidays and careers to provide our lives with joy and meaning. I thought I'd be calling you to turn away from all these to Jesus as the source of your significance.

So it was to my surprise that I discovered that the Bible paints a picture of being rightly disappointed. There can be plenty that is wrong in our disappointment, but there is also plenty that is right. It is not only understandable to feel disappointed; it is right. It is Christ-like.

We *should* be disappointed.

## THE WORLD IS DISAPPOINTING

Have you ever hated life? King Solomon did:

> So I hated life, because the work that is done under
> the sun was grievous to me. All of it is meaningless, a

chasing after the wind. I hated all the things I had toiled
for under the sun, because I must leave them to the
one who comes after me. And who knows whether that
person will be wise or foolish? Yet they will have control
over all the fruit of my toil into which I have poured my
effort and skill under the sun. This too is meaningless.
So my heart began to despair over all my toilsome
labour under the sun. For a person may labour with
wisdom, knowledge and skill, and then they must leave
all they own to another who has not toiled for it. This too
is meaningless and a great misfortune.

(Ecclesiastes 2 v 17-21)

Isn't it disappointing that we have no control over our legacy?
We might strive to build a business, a family, a reputation.
We can work hard with integrity and energy but we have no
control over what will happen after we retire, move on or die.
To think like this is disappointing. It takes the satisfaction
out of surveying the work of our hands with pride. But it is
also realistic.

Indeed, the disappointment often comes sooner than when
we confront our legacy (or lack of it). Ecclesiastes goes on to
say, "What do people get for all the toil and anxious striving
with which they labour under the sun? All their days their
work is grief and pain; even at night their minds do not rest.
This too is meaningless" (v 22-23). Our lives in this world are
full of toil and anxious striving. We don't need to survey the
fruits of our labours to feel disappointed. We simply need to
go to work! It is hard to make a living, hard to plough the
ground or satisfy a demanding boss. It is exhausting to teach
thankless children or keep pace with a production line.

We all feel disappointment—a sense that things are not as
good as they should be. And we're right to, because the world

is not as it was created to be. God created the world to be very good, but it is not what it should be. It is disappointing. Paul expresses this in Romans 8 v 18-21:

> I consider that our present sufferings are not worth comparing with the glory that will be revealed in us. For the creation waits in eager expectation for the children of God to be revealed. For the creation was subjected to frustration, not by its own choice, but by the will of the one who subjected it, in hope that the creation itself will be liberated from its bondage to decay and brought into the freedom and glory of the children of God.

One day, Jesus will come back and the creation will be freed from its current frustration and bondage. But for now, we live in a frustrated and frustrating world.

It is a strange idea to think of creation as being frustrated. We can see that it is frustrating—but frustrated? Imagine a shepherd trying to herd a flock into a pen when the sheep are bent on munching the grass and avoiding captivity. He may well find the process frustrating, but if creation is frustrated, then his sheepdog may well be sharing his frustration. Maybe the dog relishes the challenge, but the sheep probably don't. They experience frustration as their desires are thwarted. And the ripples spread wider; if the entire creation is frustrated, then (strange as it sounds) the grass must be also. I don't know whether it is frustrated to be eaten, or to be left uneaten. I am sure it is frustrated to be trampled into the mud by hooves!

Creation proclaims the glory of God (see Psalm 19); and it now proclaims the frustration of the fall. It is frustrated. In a sense, as Paul says, it experiences that frustration. I do not know how close that is to our feelings of frustration. While we share in the created-ness of creation, we are made uniquely in the image of God, and so share his capacity for affections and emotions. But the creation was created by the same Lord, and it is not immune from frustration.

When you leave the dog at home as you head out, I'm afraid that he probably really is as disappointed as he looks. Creation is frustrated, and that is a similar idea to disappointment. We see it on the face of a dog, the rebelliousness of sheep, the warping of a fence-panel, the erosion of a once-great cliff-face.

This world is disappointing. So of course we find it a frustrating place to live. Imagine you bought a new home. You'd visited the site as the houses were being put up, seen the show home, and bought off-plan. Finally the day comes when the work is finished and the developer hands over the key. You open the front door and step in to be met with the smell of freshly laid carpet and newly dried paint and sewage. Wait a moment... the plugholes shouldn't be letting that up. You go in further, and it occurs to you that the newly laid carpet shouldn't have a crease down the middle, and should reach to the other wall. Light switches should work, and the wooden work-surface shouldn't have a dent in it.

You should be disappointed by that home. If you weren't, something would be wrong. And this world is your home. So you should be disappointed. We have a divinely inbuilt sense that it should be, well, better.

When you come home from work tired and frustrated, feeling like you have got so little done, that is normal. When your holiday feels like a mixture of family rows, rain-swept beaches and just about enough snatched moments of peace to fill a small photo album, don't feel hard done by—you are not the only one on the plane home feeling that way. It is perfectly normal to be disappointed. Not only is it normal to be disappointed, it is right and realistic. You should feel disappointed.

## JESUS IS DISAPPOINTED

We are not the only ones who find the world disappointing. God is himself disappointed. This is another striking idea. It is strange to us to think of the creation as frustrated. It is perhaps even stranger to think of the Lord as disappointed.

But he is, and he was. One of the most poignant times we see this is as Jesus approaches the tomb of his friend Lazarus. Here we see the disappointment—the deep, heart-wrenching, eye-stinging, grieving disappointment—of Jesus. When he arrives at Bethany, where Lazarus had lived until his death a few days earlier, Jesus talks with Martha, one of Lazarus' sisters. Then, as he reaches their home, Mary, Lazarus' other sister, runs out to meet him:

> When Mary reached the place where Jesus was and saw him, she fell at his feet and said, "Lord, if you had been here, my brother would not have died." When Jesus saw her weeping, and the Jews who had come along with her also weeping, he was deeply moved in spirit and troubled. "Where have you laid him?" he asked.
>
> "Come and see, Lord," they replied.
>
> Jesus wept. (John 11 v 32-35)

Jesus is deeply moved in spirit and troubled at this death, and when he comes to the grave, he weeps. Here we have the eternal God shedding bitter tears over the death of his friend. Death was never meant to be part of the story, and even though Jesus knows that this particular death will be an opportunity for him to show his glory (v 4, 40), the Creator is still dismayed by its presence. Our God feels the crushing disappointment of this decaying world. And if he does, then we can too. Jesus is the most well-adjusted, spiritually-attuned, secure person who has ever lived. If he feels disappointed to the point of weeping with sadness and frustration at the world, then it is no wrong thing to feel the same way. Indeed, it is right to feel disappointed. The tears of frustration that we cry are not necessarily wrong; often they are shed in the likeness of the one who wept at Lazarus' tomb.

Jesus finds the way the world is, especially the existence of death, desperately disappointing. But it is not only the way the world is that disappoints him. It is the way people are, too. We see something of this as Jesus looks out over Jerusalem, the city of God's people that should have been overjoyed to see its Lord come:

> Jerusalem, Jerusalem, you who kill the prophets and stone those sent to you, how often I have longed to gather your children together, as a hen gathers her chicks under her wings, and you were not willing.
>
> (Luke 13 v 34)

"Often I have longed to..." That is a cry of frustration and disappointment. Surveying the city that has rejected him, Jesus laments. He must have been angry, but what we see is sorrow and frustration. He is exasperated at the stubborn refusal of so many people to enjoy his love and protection.

Jesus doesn't only feel this disappointment—he fully expects us to as well. He raised Lazarus from the dead a few moments after talking with Mary, but she and Martha had still had the pain of seeing their brother die. They wept alongside their Lord. Jesus does not insulate his friends from suffering or from disappointment. His way is the way of the cross, and he calls us to follow the same way. It is as we face up to the disappointment of this world that we get a sense of just how satisfying the salvation that we have in Christ is. If we want to live a Christ-like life in this world, then we will have to live with our eyes wide open to the disappointment in our lives and in the lives of people around us.

To feel the suffering of this world allows us to honestly and realistically hold out real hope to our family and friends who are deeply disappointed. It allows us to talk about a God who came to our world knowing how disappointing it would be, whose heart plumbed the depths of disappointment as he saw death, and as he himself suffered death, abandoned by his friends, betrayed by his people and failed by the law and society. It allows us to live like Jesus: to walk the way of the cross, and not the way of triumphalist fantasy.

## FREE TO BE DISAPPOINTED

You would be deeply disappointed in your new house if you were met by the stench of sewage as you walked into it. And we are meant to find this world deeply disappointing. If we do not, then we are settling for far too little. We were created to live day by day into all eternity in a wonderful world, full of meaning and laughter. We were made to walk among the flowering trees and flowing rivers in the garden of God. We were not made to slip over on the mud as we wrestle with a wheelie bin on a blustery, wet December morning.

There are moments—of course there are—when we glimpse the wonderful perfection of the glory of God in his creation. But there are also hours, days and years when we live with deep disappointment because nothing feels like it ought to feel. And we are right to feel so disappointed. You were not meant to go to bed lonely tonight. You were not meant to creep in exhausted from the ward. You are not meant to wake at 4am anxious about your sales target. You should not have to dread facing the bullying at school, at work, on social media. You should not know what it is to have your heart broken or your trust betrayed.

We are free to be disappointed. And we are free to be disappointed at ourselves. If Jesus is exasperated at what people are like, then I should and can be too—including with what I am like. When I shout terror into my children or snipe in bitterness at my wife, Christ is exasperated with me, and disappointed for me, that I am not living the full life he has saved me for. I can feel disappointed at myself. Strangely, this is wonderful news—because it cuts through the answers the world gives. I am told I should esteem myself and believe in myself. I should give myself a break—after all I am tired, and it's been a stressful day, and nobody is perfect.

But when I think like that, I can't be honest. I can't deal with my wife's disappointment. I have to build my walls of pride high and meet the fire of her hurt with the fire of my self-justifying fury. Once I remember I am allowed to be disappointed with myself without being crushed by it, I can simply be sad. The walls of pride are breached so that forgiveness and love can storm through.

Two nights ago I was able to apply this. In the middle of a bitter argument about birthday presents I realised that I was totally in the wrong, selfish and utterly failing to love my wife. It was freeing to be able to simply stop and say, "You're right. I'm sorry. I've been stupid."

## WHICH GOD?
The gospel of Jesus Christ presents a theology of the cross, not a theology of triumphalist glory. The way we think about God

(our theology) should be shaped and controlled by the cross. His way is to enter into the darkness of this world—to come as a man of suffering, weeping with the pain and frustration of Lazarus' death or Jerusalem's indifference. We so often want a theology of glory—a God who makes our lives glorious in our present and on our terms. We want a God who ends all our disappointments right now, who gives work, marriage, family, health, holidays, houses as though this was where real joy lay—as though we could be satisfied with these.

There is a god who will promise this. There is a god who will offer a life free from disappointment. He offered it to Eve in the fruit that hung before her in the Garden of Eden. He offered it to Jesus in the wilderness. Satan offered Christ the worship of the nations, if he would only bow the knee to him. Jesus could have had the rule without the cross. He could have had the glory of being King without the pain of being crowned with thorns. He could have had adulation without disappointment. He chose not to. He chose to obey his Father. He chose to go to his cross. He chose to feel the pain and frustration of this lost world—to become one with a lost humanity to find us, save us and bring us back to his heart and home.

This means we need to change our attitude to disappointment. If it is right to feel disappointed, if we should feel disappointed at the way our world is, then we need to stop avoiding it. We need to stop seeking the Hollywood ending. There is no magic wand and fairy dust; there is a rough cross and a suffering church. We need to stop trying to manipulate and control our world to edit out all disappointment, as though we could do in reality what is hard enough on our virtual profile.

So often we try to avoid disappointment. When we see a shocking and heartbreaking news item on the miserable plight of refugees, we pass over it so quickly. My heart is far more likely to be gripped by the new gadget, holiday or car advertised after the news. I simply avoid feeling as I should about the disappointing state of this world.

When we get home after a tough week at work, we don't think over how frustrating it is, or how normal it is to feel this way on a Friday night. Our tendency is not to linger in the disappointment. Instead we simply take it out on our family and then dodge it by putting on a film and opening a beer.

It is actually quite dangerous to be under-disappointed. It leads to us settling. We become indifferent or callous, and unable to face reality. We start thirsting for the little escapes from grinding life rather than thirsting for the world we were made for—for Eden which we will find again in the new creation. The terrible danger that Solomon confronts with bitter insight in Ecclesiastes is that we focus only on life "under the sun" and so fail to look forward to and live for our future with the Son, and fail to take seriously the reality faced by so many of a future shut out from all light.

You should be disappointed. It's very possible you should be more disappointed. Jesus was. Knowing this frees us to find the world disappointing, and ourselves disappointing, without being crushed by reality. We follow the God who walked through disappointment so that he might bring it to an end—so that he might give us hope. Jesus was not crushed by disappointment; rather, he crushed it. Before we turn there, though, we need to see that although it is right for us to feel disappointed, it is still possible to feel disappointed by the wrong things. We should weep in the world, but we should not weep as the world.

# 3. JUST TOO DISAPPOINTED

Imagine it's Saturday evening: you're in a pub in the centre of town, and your team have just lost the local derby. The mood will be sombre and irritable. (Insert the details of your team, or a loved one's team here, and imagine a thrashing by their greatest rivals, and it will ring more true!)

Most will drink a few and go home feeling low and empty—disappointed. A few will let their frustration boil over into anger, which is why there are no rival supporters anywhere near the middle of town, as the police work hard to keep opposing fans apart. They know what can happen when beer is laced with a shot of keen disappointment.

On Monday morning, when you go to work in a factory or office full of home-team fans, the mood will persist. Probably not the anger—but the disappointment will still be palpable.

So far, so unremarkable. But between Saturday night and Monday morning comes Sunday (you already knew that). If the downcast mood persists in the city's churches on a Sunday morning, then there is a problem. If the joy of a sizeable part of the congregation rests more on the victory of eleven athletes over another team than in the victory of the Son of God over death, then something is wrong.

This isn't just imagination. I know of churches where a visitor could tell the results of the Saturday afternoon match by the Sunday morning singing.

We saw in the last chapter that we're right to be disappointed—in fact, that often we should be more disappointed. But that doesn't mean our disappointment is always right. Sometimes, we are disappointed about things we really shouldn't be disappointed about at all. Perhaps more commonly, we over-react to things that are disappointing, and are *too* disappointed.

## WHAT IS DISAPPOINTMENT?

We need to back up a moment here and see what disappointment is. We all recognise and feel it, but what are we actually dealing with? Here's my definition: *disappointment is what we experience when we expect satisfaction and this satisfaction is denied.* So if you come home from a long day's work expecting your family to welcome you and they are out somewhere, you are disappointed. You expected a certain satisfaction, and it is denied.

This means that we can be rightly disappointed, as we saw in the last chapter. Often this world fails to give us the satisfaction we were created to enjoy. We shouldn't be under-disappointed about that. But we can also be over-disappointed. If we expect the wrong things to bring deep satisfaction, then we will be wrongly disappointed. Or if we expect too much satisfaction from good things, then we can be overly, and wrongly, disappointed.

## THINGS THAT SHOULDN'T DISAPPOINT US (BUT DO)

Disappointment does strange things to us when we stop to think about it. Why would a wise and respected older lady act like a jealous child when the judges award the prize for best roses to someone else one year? Why would a kind, considerate husband snap his wife's head off because his team dropped a catch at a crucial moment in the televised game? Why did I spend two hours the other Saturday refusing to communicate in more than grunts because I'd messed up on a DIY project (I'd dug the hole for the sunken trampoline too wide)?

Here's why. We have made idols of our flowers, our team, or (in my case) our DIY project. We have taken these very normal things and set them up in heaven with tin halos. We've trusted them to bring us satisfaction and we've lashed out when they disappointed us. In the days of the prophet Jeremiah, the LORD brought a terrible charge against his people:

> "Therefore I bring charges against you again,"
> declares the LORD ...
> "My people have exchanged their glorious God
>     for worthless idols.
> Be appalled at this, you heavens,
>     and shudder with great horror,"
> declares the LORD.
> "My people have committed two sins:
> They have forsaken me,
>     the spring of living water,
> and have dug their own cisterns,
>     broken cisterns that cannot hold water."
>
> (Jeremiah 2 v 11-13)

The charge is simple, and deadly serious. The people have turned away from worshipping the Lord to worship other gods. Rather than going to the temple to worship the Lord of heaven and earth, God's people are bowing down before statues that are no more than wood and stone. This is evil unfaithfulness. As the Lord has cared for his people so well, it is a wicked betrayal for them to choose other gods instead of him. It is also profoundly stupid, as these idols are "worthless". They are made of wood, stone or metal. They are not gods; they can't hear or answer prayer. They cannot help and they will not save. You may as well worship your car for all the good it would do you.

Or your new computer, or your house, or the house that you have your heart set on. Because what is a god? It is simply something that you look to to fill your life with joy, meaning, success or identity. It is your source of satisfaction. That is why, though we might not worship carved statues of ancient gods, we do worship a five-bedroom Georgian townhouse, or a powerful new BMW, or a lightning-quick phone upgrade, or an accurately measured DIY project.

In a dry land like Israel, cisterns meant life. The water they held was life, security and prosperity. A cracked cistern was not just irritating; it was life-threatening. And God is pointing out to them, and to us, that the cisterns we create for ourselves cannot hold our life. If we put our joy and contentment, our satisfaction and success into the cistern of our football team or our gardening club or our DIY project, they simply cannot hold it. Our satisfaction drains away, and all we're left with is the emptiness of disappointment.

This is why our idols leave us so disappointed. And in the cold light of day, we can see that we are silly. To put a sports team on the throne of heaven is madness. But it doesn't feel silly when we do it.

## THINGS THAT SHOULD DISAPPOINT US (BUT DO TOO MUCH)

But maybe this is not the nature of your disappointment. Perhaps your disappointment is another twenty applications submitted and not even an interview this time. Or another month gone by and the pregnancy test is negative again. Or driving away from yet another wedding with no one in the car except you. These are not silly things. This is not eleven guys being less good at kicking a sphere than eleven other guys. These are things that should disappoint us.

And yet... it is still possible for them to make us too disappointed. Wrong disappointment is not only caused by misplacing our satisfaction; it is more commonly caused by expecting too much satisfaction from things that are good, and so experiencing disappointment that is disproportionate to the situation. This is harder to spot, because the thing that is disappointing to us can be serious, and something that should rightly make us feel deeply disappointed. It's hard to work out when right disappointment has tipped over into over-disappointment.

One way we can spot this over-blown disappointment is when it becomes the "but..." at the end of every good thing. It's the negative that colours every positive in life in a shade of grey. You have a great holiday, but every memory is tinged with sadness that you are single when you long to be married.

Imagine you're talking to a friend who has just got back from a weekend away with some old school friends:

"How was your weekend?"

"Well, it was good, thanks. The cottage was lovely, and the weather on Saturday was just right. We all had a long walk together along the coast, then lit a fire. Daniel had cooked a feast for the evening, and it was great to catch up. I can't believe it is two years since we were all together—it felt like last week. It was a great weekend, but..."

"Sounds really lovely. Sorry, I interrupted. You were going to say something else...?"

"Well, Phil and Natalie are clearly so happy, and I'm really pleased for them, of course, but... I just hoped I'd be married by now, you know? And Daniel's living the dream with that new manager's job, and it's lovely to see him so content, but...it did remind me that I don't think I'll ever get a break. I think I'll go mad if I can't get a better job soon. Then, Doug and Amy are pretty nervous about having twins, obviously! But I'd take those nerves any day—I'll be 34 next month and can't imagine meeting anyone, let alone having a family."

Nothing can be good, nothing can satisfy. There is always a "but..." at the end of all the joy and goodness, and the "but" overshadows and comes to overwhelm all the joy and goodness. It often comes out in comparisons with our friends. This is not simple jealousy, though; it is the subtler disappointment of what they have highlighting what we lack. What has happened? We have made something that we are right to regret the lack of into a god without which we cannot enjoy life. We have poured the water of our life into a broken cistern—marriage, career, family, house, whatever, and it cannot hold it. It cannot be our life.

It's worth asking yourself, *Who am I?* I, John, am a whole collection of identities. I am a husband, a father, a son, a friend. But most of all, I am a child of God through what Christ achieved on the cross. And if the core of my identity is not in being a child of God, then I will tend to make something, or more often someone, my god. If I do not find my ultimate satisfaction in Christ, I will make the person I do find it in my idol. And that person is not a god, and so will not satisfy me.

The key issue is what goes before and after the "but" in your life. You can say, for example, "I am a follower of Christ, but I cannot have children and so life will be dominated by disappointment", or you can run it the other way around: "I cannot have children, but I am loved by God and there is joy in him". The question is where the weight lies. Either way there is disappointment; but we can define our life by disappointment or we can define our life by Jesus. The first is an indication of idolatry; the second is a sign of real, hope-filled faith.

## THE PROBLEM OF SUCCESS

There is one more area of disappointment that can be more crushing than a lack of something, more crushing than a failure at something. It is the disappointment of success.

I turned 40 last week, and a lot of my friends of a similar age are desperately disappointed with their successful lives. Picture a family living in a decent house. The mum and dad both have jobs; he is a teacher and she is a nurse—the work they trained to do nearly twenty years ago now. Their kids are 13 and 9, and doing well at school. They've booked a nice holiday on the beach, and are off to visit the grandparents this weekend. They are enjoying all they have worked for and all that they dreamed of when they first got together.

Except they're not. Enjoying it, that is. Driving home from a night shift, Anna pulls in for a coffee and wonders if this is really it. Paul is a good bloke, and she knows she has nothing to grumble about really... but married life is so predictable, so routine. She loves the kids, but she is fed up with the washing, the cleaning, the complaining. She knows the holiday will be fun, but she longs for the days when they travelled. There is nothing wrong, and that's part of the problem. There's nothing wrong, and yet it doesn't feel like she thought it would. And because nothing's wrong, she's not sure how to put it right.

It is the same for Paul. Later in the day, halfway through marking a pile of books on the kitchen table, he wonders if he can really stand another 25 years of this. He feels like he's going mad inside, and understands what makes blokes jack it all in. A mid-life crisis would at least be more interesting than marking homework, he thinks to himself with a smile. Anna looks tired as she gets the supper ready and he wonders why. He knows he looks the same, but has no idea why. Life has just lost its fun and its shine.

Paul and Anna are successful. Their marriage, family life, home, jobs and even their holiday mark them out as successful. But there is a quiet, unnamed, almost unnoticed desperation there. Such success in life does not satisfy. If it did, we would never read stories of celebrities who have it all choosing to throw it all away in the drink, drugs or divorces that hit the headlines. It is just as true in "normal" success.

Isn't that strange? We have everything we wanted, but it still feels empty. We should be satisfied but we aren't. We're just quietly, and sometimes desperately, disappointed.

The collapse that lies down this road might be less spectacular than for the celebrities. It may simply look like giving up to sadness, depression and apathy. It might look like getting out—leaving the marriage, moving house or taking some other radical action. It might merely look like temporary escapes—immersing ourselves in the amazingly detailed plots and characterisations of modern TV, or in simple old-fashioned booze or shopping. Or the quiet disappointment might make us angry, in a slow, bone-rotting way that boils to the surface sometimes in the spitting fury of the person old enough to know better.

## THE DANGER OF OVER-DISAPPOINTMENT

This is the danger of over-disappointment. When we have no hope because we have made silly things or good things into idols, then we despair. And in people, despair looks ugly. It looks ugly because it never stays in one person; it spreads and touches all our relationships.

I was going to write that when I have had a disappointing day, I struggle to treat my wife with kindness and gentleness and my children with patience. That isn't true. I don't struggle. I don't even attempt to fight the overflow of disappointment.

Disappointment that is allowed to fester over time leads to bitterness and misery. It can come out in distance—the husband who lives in his shed because he can't confront his marriage any longer, or the woman who buries herself in work because it's too much to be reminded of how her friends are coupled up, and she isn't.

Very often, though, it comes out in anger. I think a lot of this is hidden in families. The arguments of tired mums and dads with the hurt and pain they inflict are often the overflow of bitter disappointment. So is the unrestrained anger poured out on children over a little thing they have done, or not done. When there is a reservoir of bitterness, resentment and over-disappointment, it only takes a small crack to burst the dam that usually holds it all back. Sometimes the consequences are controllable, and at other times not, as words fail and fists take over. Sometimes the consequences are irreparable—the affair, the divorce, the debts, the catastrophic career change.

## THE FIRST STEP

So how can we change? How can we get perspective on our wrong disappointment, so that we feel the disappointment we should, but don't let it become all-consuming? How can I be sad about the way my career got stuck without making a promotion my god? How do I see myself as a child of God who would love a more interesting 9-5, rather than seeing myself only as a guy who never made it at work?

The good news is that we can repent. Strangely, seeing that over-disappointment is idolatry, and therefore is sin, is constructive—because you can do something about this. You can repent. That's the first step.

The first of the Ten Commandments is simple: "You shall have no other gods before me" (Exodus 20 v 3). The greatest commandment identified by Jesus puts this positively: "Love the Lord your God with all your heart and with all your soul and with all your mind" (Matthew 22 v 37). This means we can turn away from our over-disappointment and turn to an absolutely satisfying love for God.

We can stop trying to drink from an empty cistern and come to the real source of water.

Or, to put it another way, we can turn away from crushing, dominating disappointment by magnifying God. The next three chapters will show us how God both helps us root out wrong disappointment and cut back right disappointment. They will show us how to magnify, enlarge and truly see the Lord, and so see our disappointments in the light of his greater glory.

You can't kill disappointment. Often, as we've seen, you shouldn't. But you do need to keep your disappointment in perspective. You do need to shrink your over-disappointment back to the right size. To do this, you need a right view of the goodness, greatness, generosity and glory of God. You need to magnify the Lord.

In the end, it is a question of perspective. A couple of friends couldn't make my wedding day. I guess it was a bit of a shame, but to be honest, I didn't even notice. My eyes were fixed on the most delightful woman I have met, and my mind was full of the wonder that she was actually choosing to be my bride. Yes, I wish those friends had made it. But it would have been strange, rude, and wrong of me to walk round with Flick on my arm, thinking, "I wish John and Kirsty were here. This is all great, but it's not really much good without John and Kirsty here. I wonder if Flick would ring John and Kirsty and see if we can get them here."

We have a great husband, lover, friend, Lord, King and God in Jesus Christ. If our eyes are fixed on him, the disappointments we feel are kept in perspective. They are real. They may be keenly felt. But they are not the last word. They do not dictate our emotions.

## THE FREEDOM OF THANKFULNESS

So how do we magnify the Lord? We do so by being thankful. Thankfulness is a powerful defence, and that can define us rather than disappointment. But how can we be thankful when we feel disappointed? When we are disappointed with success, it is simple (although surprisingly hard to do). Rather than asking if this is it, we can just give thanks to God for what we have. More powerfully, though, we can learn to thank God for who he is and what he has done for us, rather than tying our thankfulness to the circumstances we face today.

If we look to Christ, we are thankful. We see his death for us, and his promise to return in glory and raise us from the dead, ending all suffering and disappointment... and we magnify him. This makes it easier for us to give thanks for what he might be doing in our circumstances.

When Mary, pregnant with Jesus, goes to visit her relative Elizabeth, she does not focus on what it might mean for an unmarried woman to have a child. She does not gaze at the uncertainties, the taint of scandal, the lost youth. Instead she declares, "My soul magnifies the Lord, and my spirit rejoices in God my Saviour" (Luke 1 v 46, ESV). Because her soul magnifies God, she sees the circumstances and the costs in the light of his plans and love, rather than the other way around.

When you magnify Christ, you become thankful. And when you are thankful, it magnifies Christ. It makes him bigger in your life: closer to the size, weight and significance he should have. It doesn't stop you being disappointed, but it changes it. It will extinguish some disappointments— after all, it really is only a football match. It will shrink other disappointments—however good the possession, the relationship or whatever it is you lack, it would never have borne the weight of your life or given you the satisfaction that is found only in God. Thankfulness will increase your joy, not so that disappointments are no longer part of your life, but so that they are crowded out by the One who gives you life— life to the full, and life for ever. We will see more of how this happens in the next three chapters. But the crucial antidote to over-disappointment is simply: to learn to say with Mary:

My soul magnifies the Lord, and my spirit rejoices in God my Saviour, for...

# 4. HOPE THAT DESTROYS DESPAIR

Disappointment is murky. It is dark and elusive. To try to take hold of it is like trying to stamp on a cockroach. We used to have the occasional cockroach in our last house. Sometimes you'd come downstairs and turn on the light and see one scuttle away. It still makes me shudder (I am squeamish by nature). The only good thing was that they didn't like the light. They would scuttle into the corners.

Well, now it is time to drive disappointment to the corners with a light so bright that one day it will drive disappointment clean out of our lives.

## THE CONCLUSION OF THE MATTER

Let's go back to Ecclesiastes. As we've seen, it is a study of disappointment. We're going to jump to the end, to see the "conclusion of the matter".

> Not only was the Teacher wise, but also he imparted
> knowledge to the people. He pondered and searched out
> and set in order many proverbs. The Teacher searched to

find just the right words, and what he wrote was upright and true.

The words of the wise are like goads, their collected sayings like firmly embedded nails—given by one shepherd. Be warned, my son, of anything in addition to them.

Of making many books there is no end, and much study wearies the body.

Now all has been heard;
    here is the conclusion of the matter:
fear God and keep his commandments,
    for this is the duty of all mankind.
For God will bring every deed into judgment,
    including every hidden thing,
    whether it is good or evil. (Ecclesiastes 12 v 9-14)

There is an affirmation that the book is right. This section is the conclusion to the whole book, standing back from the body of writing to assess it. It concludes that this is wisdom. The Teacher was wise, and so you can trust that these words about disappointment come from God. Ecclesiastes is not in the Bible by mistake, or to show you how not to think. Ecclesiastes is in the Bible to show us how to take our disappointment to God.

The conclusion also tells us how it does that. "The words of the wise are like goads." A goad was a sharp stick that a herder would use to prod an animal to make it go the right way. Ecclesiastes is not a book of answers; it is a book of questions. It is a sharp stick that is meant to make us feel uncomfortable as it pricks us into the right path.

Solomon drives us to God, goads us to God, by taking life

to its terrible, desperately disappointing conclusion. Not only is this life meaningless, but at the end of it we die. In fact, it is because we die that life is so meaningless. That is the subject of the first part of chapter 12. It is a mournful, yearning poem on the end of life, when "...the golden bowl is broken ... and the spirit returns to God who gave it".

The poem ends with a final cry of meaninglessness. The meaninglessness of life is sealed in death. We are disappointed, and then we die, and there is no resolution— no answer except a final cry of "Meaningless!" echoing into the eternal darkness. Even the good we have done—the scraps of meaning we have sown together—are mocked by our death. Who knows whether those who come after us will be wise or foolish? Solomon was wise to think like this—his own son would see most of his kingdom torn from his hand, partly through Solomon's own mistakes. The great empire of Solomon, built on the wisdom of God, was gone within a matter of months.

Yet Solomon has not finished. He has still not reached the conclusion of the matter. Only if we grapple with the hard reality of life and harsh finality of death are we ready to appreciate the wonder of the hope. It is as we feel that life sucks, and wonder if there is any point at all, that we can properly grasp hope. Death is not the end. We are to "fear God and keep his commandments, for this is the duty of all mankind.. Why? "For God will bring every deed into judgment, including every hidden thing, whether it is good or evil."

There is a judgment after death. Initially this seems to simply make things worse. Great, we think—we live a life full of disappointment, and then we are forced to come before God and that dreary life is laid out in all its humiliating mediocrity. How, well, disappointing. But wait. There are two ways that the judgment of God over our lives is very good news when we are faced with disappointment.

## LOOKING FORWARD TO JUDGMENT

Think of Solomon's legacy. Did it all get destroyed by his son Rehoboam? No. No, because God saw the work that he did, and God judges every deed. He will judge the wisdom of Solomon as wise. Christ will look at the good Solomon did and declare it good. In a shining shaft of light the judgment of all things by Jesus suddenly restores, and amplifies a thousand-fold, the meaning that we thought was lost.

God's judgment means that how you live—how you speak, think and act—matters. It is not meaningless, even if it seems to achieve nothing now. If you persevere through the hard and bitter times of life and it seems that there is no meaning, no satisfaction, you need to look forward. The good you have done will receive recognition and affirmation from Christ. He will look at your life—the ways you held on to him despite the disappointment in your marriage, family, work or church and he will catch your eye, smiling as he says, "Well done, good and faithful servant". Then you will know, and know for the rest of eternity, that it was not meaningless! There is more satisfaction in the smile of Jesus than there is disappointment in a thousand lifetimes.

So disappointment scurries into the corners. It is disappointing that you have never succeeded in your work as you hoped you would, but your faithful toil is judged as success in the eyes of Christ. Your bosses judged you as a failure for forty years, maybe, but when Christ declares that you worked faithfully for him, that judgment will stand for eternity and echo through countless ages. The judgment of Christ, the great Judge, gives us hope when we are disappointed by all the little judgments passed on us along the way. This world and your heart may conspire to tell you that you are nothing and life passed you by. But it may well be that Jesus is seeing your life very differently. And it is his verdict that echoes to eternity.

This is one of the reasons why obeying Christ is such an attractive way to live. He has told us how to live in a way that will meet with a divine hand clapped on our backs and a divine voice warmly greeting us: "Well done, good and faithful servant". It is an incredible thought that the glorious King of creation who sustains every star and controls every comet sees your obedience and is ready to declare that you have done well. A day spent obeying Christ need never be a disappointing day because it will be revealed and praised on the final day.

## JUDGMENT AND THE REMOVAL OF YOUR DISAPPOINTMENT

What about when we give in to the despair, though? What about the times we do not persevere or live with faith despite the disappointment? What about when the prospect of Jesus' welcome and embrace do not cause us to live in obedience, and the feeling of desperate disappointment provokes us to live in outright disobedience? For sinners like you and me, surely there the coming judgment of God is a cause for more despair, rather than for hope? It might end meaninglessness, but it will end us too. The judgment of Christ is not an attractive prospect when even I, who am so quick to find excuses, think that many of my deeds are shabby and selfish. The hidden things of my life are far more full of shame and sin than obedience and kindness. I do not want them exposed. I do not want them judged.

And they will not be. Not in the sense of being condemned and punished. If you are a follower of Jesus, the day when that happens lies behind you, not ahead of you. Judgment Day has already happened for you. When the great first-generation Christian missionary Paul preached in Athens, he called his hearers to repent, to turn back to God, with the promise that God, "has set a day when he will judge the world with justice by the man he has appointed. He has given proof of this to everyone by raising him from the dead" (Acts 17 v 31).

Our Judge is our sin-bearing, death-defeating, risen Saviour. He knew more disappointment than you ever will—he experienced the total rejection of the people he had made, and the utter meaninglessness of the outer darkness of hell. He did that for you. He died in our place; he was judged in our place. He did this for us, and he broke the power of our sin and our death. Jesus died and as he did so, he destroyed death. He broke its hold over us. On the third day after they killed him, Jesus walked out of his grave. He rose to life again: to indestructible, unending, glorious life. And he shares that life with us. Those people whose sin he carried, whose disappointment he owned, whose death he died—those people will live with him.

When Jesus comes back to judge, he will find no sin in your life if you are his follower. He has taken it all and killed it all. When he comes back to judge, he will declare you innocent, righteous, justified. And you will rise with him; you will rise to life again—indestructible, unending, glorious life. Death is not the end. This world is not all there is. The conclusion of the matter is that there will be a day when Jesus judges us, and that renders important all we do, and that assures us that our eternity is secure. And this conclusion is the stick that Christ uses to goad us into broad pastures and sun-drenched valleys.

## DOWNCAST FACES AND RESURRECTION LIFE

We can see the difference the rising of Christ from the dead makes to our lives if we consider the disciples who met him on the road to Emmaus on the day he rose, but who did not know it was him:

> [Jesus] asked them, "What are you discussing together as you walk along?"
>
> They stood still, their faces downcast. One of them, named Cleopas, asked him, "Are you the only one visiting Jerusalem who does not know the things that have happened there in these days?"
>
> "What things?" he asked.
>
> "About Jesus of Nazareth," they replied. "He was a prophet, powerful in word and deed before God and all the people. The chief priests and our rulers handed him over to be sentenced to death, and they crucified him; but we had hoped that he was the one who was going to redeem Israel. And what is more, it is the third day since all this took place. In addition, some of our women amazed us. They went to the tomb early this morning but didn't find his body. They came and told us that they had seen a vision of angels, who said he was alive. Then some of our companions went to the tomb and found it just as the women had said, but they did not see Jesus."
>
> He said to them, "How foolish you are, and how slow to believe all that the prophets have spoken! Did not the Messiah have to suffer these things and then enter his glory?" And beginning with Moses and all the Prophets, he explained to them what was said in all the Scriptures concerning himself.

As they approached the village to which they were going, Jesus continued on as if he were going further. But they urged him strongly, "Stay with us, for it is nearly evening; the day is almost over." So he went in to stay with them.

When he was at the table with them, he took bread, gave thanks, broke it and began to give it to them. Then their eyes were opened and they recognised him, and he disappeared from their sight. They asked each other, "Were not our hearts burning within us while he talked with us on the road and opened the Scriptures to us?"

They got up and returned at once to Jerusalem. There they found the Eleven and those with them, assembled together and saying, "It is true! The Lord has risen and has appeared to Simon." Then the two told what had happened on the way, and how Jesus was recognised by them when he broke the bread. (Luke 24 v 17-35)

Their faces were downcast, their hearts filled with the misery of hopes dashed to splinters. They had thought that Jesus was the one who would free their people. Now all they had was the empty disappointment of his death.

*Then they saw Jesus.* He broke bread at the supper table and their eyes were opened to see that death was not the end, that Christ was risen. Disappointment is not the end; the hope of the resurrection heralds its death.

It was not just joy that filled their lives when they saw Jesus, though. Their hearts burned as he showed them the wonder of the resurrection in the Scriptures. This is important for us, because it shows us how the hope of the resurrection works its way back through the ages. One day we will see Jesus with our own eyes, just as they did. One day you will look into the face of the One who made you, saved you and loves you more deeply than you can imagine. Today, though, you can see him with the eyes of faith. You can read the wonder of the resurrection in the Bible and let that allow you to live in joy—a life where the dominant note is not one of disappointment but of hope.

The perspective of the resurrection changes the nature of right disappointment. The longings that you have are so often right, and the lack of meaning in this life is a terrible tragedy. I don't know how each of these longings will be satisfied in the new creation, when we experience resurrection, but I know they will be.

We so often find life in this world disappointing because we were not made for this world. We were not created for a world of sin and death; we were created to walk in the garden in the cool of the day face to face with our God. We were created for a fulfilling world, not a futile world—for a generous and expansive world, not a limited and broken one. And the resurrected Jesus declares that we will spend by far the greater part of our lives in that world. We will rise from the dead to live in that world when Christ returns. We may not even die if he comes back first, but we will be changed, and everything will be different. When we see Jesus' face, we will not be disappointed. He will wipe away all those frustrated tears, and all those disappointed sobs, and he will smile. Then he will usher us into his joy, to share his wonder and laughter, to know the meaning of being with him and with his Father and ours for all eternity.

## HE IS NEVER DISAPPOINTING

You see, Jesus is never disappointing. He is never cold or empty or failing to satisfy. Whatever hopes and dreams you have, whatever yearnings and longings of the heart, you will find them all satisfied in Christ. Indeed, you will find that your cup overflows. This is a Bible image (in places like Psalm 23 v 5) that we can rush past. But the picture is powerful. You are at a feast, holding out your wine-cup to the host. He grabs a bottle and slops the fine vintage in, and he just keeps going. "Whoa there!" you say, as the wine sloshes out of your cup and down your arm. He pours it all over the place and smiles, gesturing to the groaning racks across the room. He has more than enough!

Jesus is so full of joy, hope, laughter and meaning that he sloshes it about freely. He can fill whatever emptiness you have; however big the cup, his endless supply will keep it spilling everywhere for eternity. No, Jesus is never disappointing.

We talked in the last chapter of the tendency for every good thing to end with a "but...". Disappointment does that. It robs the good of its goodness. The resurrection of Christ does just the opposite. It adds a far larger "but" to every disappointment. Take the imaginary conversation from the last chapter:

"Well, Phil and Natalie are clearly so happy, and I'm really pleased for them, of course, but... I just hoped I'd be married by now, you know? And Daniel's living the dream with that new manager's job, and it's lovely to see him so content, but...it did remind me that I don't think I'll ever get a break. I think I'll go mad if I can't get a better job soon. Then, Doug and Amy are pretty nervous about having twins, obviously! But I'd take those nerves any day—I'll be 34 next month and can't imagine meeting anyone, let alone having a family."

That isn't how it ends for the Christian. It ends like this:

"... I'll be 34 next month and maybe Jesus will have returned first. Then we will be his Bride, and I guess Phil and Natalie's joy is just a trailer for ours then. Daniel's job is good, but he isn't really living the dream, unless he is managing heavenly constellations of course, but I'm pretty sure it's just the southeast region. Then I'll be ruling all things with my Jesus. I don't know how he's going to fulfil my longing for children, but he's made promises, and a God who died for me and rose to give me life is one I'm going to trust."

It all ends with a "but". *But* Jesus is alive. *But* Jesus is coming back. *But* there is hope. You will be judged by your Saviour, who has already taken the punishment for your failures, including the times when you should have been disappointed by pain and the world and yourself and were not, and the times when you were over-disappointed by good things you had chosen to worship in his place. You will be judged by your Saviour, who will welcome you with words of joyful approval for the moments of quiet obedience that no one else noticed or cared about. There is never a need to despair. Yes, disappointment is real, and it is powerful. But it is not as real and powerful as Jesus. He is full of life, joy peace and hope. He is risen. He is alive. He is coming back. For you.

# 5. PURPOSE THAT CUTS OFF ESCAPE

The man sits at his office desk, bored out of his mind. He absent-mindedly plays with a mascot sitting by his computer; it's an old childhood toy—one of the droids from the Star Wars films. In his mind, he's back playing Star Wars with his friend as a boy—fighting with his lightsabre torch, riding his bike pretending to be a flying star fighter. He is brought back to the humdrum reality of his office by a roaring noise... his childhood friend is outside the window—in an X-Wing star fighter! A second spaceship rises alongside, with canopy open and seat empty. The office-worker immediately throws his chair through the window and jumps into the cockpit, and they race off together to save the galaxy.

As adverts for computer games go, this is a great one (it certainly appeals to me!). And it is a revealing one too. It plays on the assumption that most men in their thirties want to escape their lives. As children they dreamed of saving the galaxy (or something equally exciting); and as adults they save people 10% on their car insurance. It's not exactly on a par with flying a star fighter!

The disappointment is not simply that childhood dreams were dreams, though. You knew (probably) that you would never fly a star fighter, but you did hope that your life would feel as exciting, stimulating and meaningful as if you did fly one. But of course, life didn't pan out that way. So the man sits in his office and he escapes into his daydreams—because in reality there is no friend in a star fighter. There is only the next caller.

## A GREAT ESCAPE

> I amassed silver and gold for myself, and the treasure of kings and provinces. I acquired male and female singers, and a harem as well—the delights of a man's heart. I became greater by far than anyone in Jerusalem before me. In all this my wisdom stayed with me.
>
> I denied myself nothing my eyes desired;
>     I refused my heart no pleasure.
> My heart took delight in all my labour,
>     and this was the reward for all my toil.
> Yet when I surveyed all that my hands had done
>     and what I had toiled to achieve,
> everything was meaningless, a chasing after the wind;
>     nothing was gained under the sun.
>
> (Ecclesiastes 2 v 8-11)

Sooner or later, we wonder what the point is—and struggle to find any purpose at all, or at least any purpose that death doesn't mock. And the more we amass or experience, the more elusive "purpose" becomes. Solomon had tried lots of things—wealth, music, women, pleasure, beauty, fame, work. He denied himself nothing. Yet still, "everything was meaningless". What is sobering about Ecclesiastes is that there is virtually no escape route from meaninglessness that Solomon had left untried and untrodden.

Wrestling with a sense of purpose is unique to humanity. Rabbits don't sit around wondering why they are here. Eagles don't hover in the sky seeking some point to it all. We do. And when we do, we find purpose elusive. That's why, to differing extents and in different ways, we all tend to seek to escape from the humdrum of life in the hope of discovering the exciting, purpose-filled existence that we feel we ought to have but find so hard to enjoy.

Having a mid-life crisis is a cliché for a reason—it's often a reality. For some, it involves a complete change of jobs. For others it's taking up a new hobby, or re-engaging with an old one. Or in a much more extreme and painful version, the wife and family are changed rather than the leisure pursuit or career. Several friends of mine have got divorced in the last couple of years. I'm not sure they really know why. There are many reasons given, but even they don't find them particularly compelling. I certainly don't want to reduce the reasons for everything to disappointment leading to escapism, but as I listen to my friends, I sense that it played its part, at least.

Others do not totally change their lives; they simply create an alter-ego. I think this is often what is going on in an affair. When you are with someone who doesn't know you—who doesn't see your socks poking out of the laundry basket or what you look like when you've got flu—you can be anyone. Ever-present technology brings alter-ego escapism much closer to home. Why would I be a supermarket customer services manager when I can be a star-fighter pilot? Why would I slog through my list of dull chores when I can update my profile with selected photos and quips and become a stellar mum?

Life can be so much more interesting as a series of tweets than a series of minutes.

Perhaps the most common way we escape, though, is not to create an alter-ego, but to live for short moments and just get through the rest. I have friends who book their next holiday the moment they get home. They constantly talk about holidays; they have the photos on their screensaver and on their walls. They truly live in those two, three or four weeks a year, and the rest of the time is just in-between time, doing what must be done to get back to the beach, the ski slopes or the trail.

Or maybe we do the same week by week, using entertainment as our escape. The next episode can become the exciting part of life, the purpose of the day just to get through the 9-5, get the kids to bed, and then put the box set on. If I have an evening in by myself, I will probably open a beer and put on one of the *Lord of the Rings* films (I have the extended editions!). I want to spend my evening immersed in a fight of good against evil conducted by bow and sword. Being a king of Gondor, elf or hobbit is just so much more interesting than my life. The highlight of my weekend easily becomes the film I saw on Saturday night, not the Jesus I saw on Sunday night.

Another form of escape is one that at first seems a dark admission of the disappointment of life rather than an escape from it. Some of us turn to the bottle or to drugs, gambling, pornography or other addictive and potentially self-destructive activities. Even here there is an escape. It may look as if this is simply dulling our awareness of the disappointment, but there is a reordering of life, and a quest for purpose and significance that is not found in the normal course of life. Searching for purpose in the darkness of drunkenness, sexual perversion or high-risk addiction is not strange if there is none to be found elsewhere. Even a temporary high can give a sense of purpose if that is the only place where purpose can be found. At some point it will become clear that there is certainly no more purpose in the darkness than in the light, but if one as wise as Solomon trod this path (e.g. Ecclesiastes 2 v 10), we should not be surprised that we find it so attractive.

Our attempts to escape amount to the same thing. Following Solomon in a desperate pursuit of purpose, we find only meaninglessness. Every escape hatch leads to a dead end. Yet most of us refuse to accept that it must be like this—that a despairing acceptance of meaninglessness is the final answer. And that's good—it's always very sad to meet someone who has accepted despair because they've stopped looking for any purpose or point. That's not life; that's just existence.

And the great news, however you're escaping and even if you're despairing, is that you don't need to. There is a purpose to be found in ordinary life, even one of sitting in an office selling car insurance. Let me show you what that is.

## AND THE POINT OF LIFE IS...

It's easy to think of the Christian life as an escapist one. If our real life starts when the risen Christ returns, then isn't the Christian just waiting for that, treading water till he returns or calls us home to heaven? Some people book their holiday for next summer and then slog through to it; by faith in Christ our eternity is secure and we're slogging through to it.

But that's to ignore love.

Jesus' purpose in life was very clear, and equally simple. It was to glorify his Father by showing love, ultimately by "humbling himself by becoming obedient to death" (Philippians 2 v 8). He wants his followers to enjoy the same, infinitely wonderful, purpose. Just before he is arrested and killed, Jesus prays for his followers—for those of us who are Christians:

> Father, the hour has come. Glorify your Son, that your Son may glorify you. For you granted him authority over all people that he might give eternal life to all those you have given him. Now this is eternal life: that they know you, the only true God, and Jesus Christ, whom you have sent. (John 17 v 1-3)

Christ has given us, his followers, eternal life. This life is not a matter of breathing or moving only; it is a matter of relationship. Eternal life is to know God our Father and his Son. This is possible because Christ gives the Spirit to us. The Holy Spirit comes to give us an unending spring of life within ourselves (John 4 v 14; 7 v 38-39). To have eternal life is to live in intimate relationship with the Trinity, part of the family of God. It is to have God as your Father, Christ as your Brother and the Spirit in your heart. To have eternal life is to be loved by God and to love him. And that starts now.

This love then flows out to others. The ministry of Jesus is full of this, from the two great commandments to love God and then to love one another (Matthew 22 v 37-40) to his giving of a new commandment in John 13 v 34-35:

> A new command I give you: love one another. As I have loved you, so you must love one another. By this everyone will know that you are my disciples, if you love one another.

The purpose of this life is to be loved and to love. This is what we were created for by God in the beginning and this is what we have been born again for. The purpose of our eternal life is not to achieve great things; it is not to be faster, higher or stronger; it is not to increase in wealth, fame or popularity. It is to be loved and to love.

This may sound off-putting, though—disappointing even. Is this really the great purpose? Be loved, and love? If this is your thought, then it's probably because "love" is a word that has a huge range of meanings. And maybe for you love means taking a risk and getting hurt. Or maybe for you love conjures up images of teddy bears and flowers and pet-names and debating who will hang up the phone next, and you have had enough of that soppy sentimentality.

Well, that's not at all what the Bible calls "love". The love that the Bible holds up is the love of Christ on the cross. It fights. It is passionate. It is sincere. It is brave. It is strong. It is courageous. It is committed. It will give anything—even life—for its beloved.

To love is to live as Jesus lives. It is to show and share the good news of his kingdom. It is to treat all with compassion and kindness while pointing all to Christ and speaking freely of his greater love. It is to joyfully forget yourself, give yourself, sacrifice yourself. It is to love those who persecute you, praying for them as Christ did for the men who nailed his hands to the cross, blessing them as he did when he made Saul the killer into Paul the preacher. It is to count your life here as of little value because you have an eternal life of infinitely greater duration and worth. It is to take up your cross and love others as Christ loves them, and you.

## REAL PURPOSE

The wonder of the eternal resurrection life that Jesus gives us is that we have this love, right now, in the ordinariness of our days. We do not need to escape to seek it. It does not reside in an alter ego or rely on the power of our imagination. It's real.

And it gives us purpose. When Christ returns, my exam certificates will burn, my bank balance will be worthless and my fame will be inconsequential. But love will endure. Paul talks about this in 1 Corinthians 3 v 10-15, comparing our life's work to a building:

> By the grace God has given me, I laid a foundation as a wise builder, and someone else is building on it. But each one should build with care. For no one can lay any foundation other than the one already laid, which is Jesus Christ. If anyone builds on this foundation using gold, silver, costly stones, wood, hay or straw, their work will be shown for what it is, because the Day will bring it to light. It will be revealed with fire, and the fire will test the quality of each person's work. If what has been built survives, the builder will receive a reward. If it is burned up, the builder will suffer loss but yet will be saved— even though only as one escaping through the flames.

The only thing that endures through the judgment of Christ is people. So the only work that will endure is the work we have done in the lives of those around us. Our love is all that will remain on the day of judgment. Nothing else. Paul returns to this theme even more powerfully in chapter 13. When all else fails, it is love that will endure into all eternity:

> Love never fails. But where there are prophecies, they will cease; where there are tongues, they will be stilled; where there is knowledge, it will pass away. For we know in part and we prophesy in part, but when completeness comes, what is in part disappears ... And now these three remain: faith, hope and love. But the greatest of these is love. (1 Corinthians 13 v 8-10, 13)

Disappointment is ongoing, and so only love can establish meaning in the face of disappointment, because love precedes it and will outlive it. We were loved before creation (John 17 v 24, 26). People endure beyond this age, so love will always have eternal significance.

Sometimes, we cannot see how this is. That is because you and I are not God. Picture a mighty cathedral, built over many decades, stretching to a couple of centuries. None of the workmen who dug the foundations saw the cross being hoisted to the top of the spire. Maybe they do not even know what they are helping to build. They only know that their purpose is to dig, and they do that diligently, knowing they're engaged on something bigger and more glorious than themselves. You may not see the results of your love. You may share the gospel with a loved one out of deep love for them, and see it rejected again and again. You may serve someone selflessly and receive no thanks or even recognition. But God says that love always has a purpose—that it is building with gold. He is the master builder, and love is the material with which he builds. Love is the only way we can build eternally sturdy structures. It is only the love that we show which will endure, because only people endure.

Loving doesn't just change the beloved. It changes the lover too. To love is to live like our God, and so loving makes us more like Jesus. If I love a friend who never responds to Christ's love, then I have still built with gold, because the good done in my life will endure. When I love, I build gold in my life as well perhaps as in that of my friend. The aim of love is selfless, to bless others, but the result of selfless love is my growth in Christ-likeness. Jesus died for his church because he loved his Father and loved us. When you love, you are being like him, living like him, and becoming more like him.

When our friend in his car insurance office loves a caller he will never meet by making sure they are able to steward their money in the best way possible, or spotting an area of insurance cover they need and have not noticed, or responding gently and generously to a tirade, he is becoming more like the Creator and Saviour of the world, and more like the person he himself was created and saved to be. Which is always better and infinitely more satisfying than letting his colleague take the call because he's staring out of the window hoping that maybe, just maybe, the star-fighter will show up.

## THE POSSIBLE IMPOSSIBILITY OF LOVE

There is only one problem in all of this. You and I find love impossible. Let's consider the closest relationships in life—our family or close friends. In one sense, I can say that I always love my wife and children. In another sense, I really can't say that. Watch a day in the Hindley household and you'll almost certainly see me snapping, using unkind words, ducking out of jobs that would help the others, and so on. I cannot make myself love even those I most love!

Which is terrible, but also liberating, because it shows me that I can only love by the power of the Spirit. Love is part of the fruit of the Spirit (Galatians 5 v 22)—it's a characteristic that God himself grows in us as we "keep in step with the Spirit". I do not need to make myself love my wife and children (and everyone else) in my own strength; but I do need to work at it as I rely on God's help. What is impossible for me to achieve alone becomes the simple gift of God to me, for me to unwrap.

The apostle John explains in a famous, wonderful passage both what love is and what love does:

This is love: not that we loved God, but that he loved us and sent his Son as an atoning sacrifice for our sins. Dear friends, since God so loved us, we also ought to love one another. No one has ever seen God; but if we love one another, God lives in us and his love is made complete in us. (1 John 4 v 10-12)

The gold standard of love is not primarily what I show to others; it is what I receive from God. Love is not defined by my love for others, but by his love for me, seen in his Son dying on a cross because he was so determined to give his people eternal life that he would bear any cost to achieve it. And when we look at that love, the Spirit helps us to show that love—and when we do, we give people a glimpse of the Father whom no one has ever seen.

The divine orchestra began playing a symphony of love before the minor key music of disappointment began, and it will keep playing after disappointment ends, but at the moment, we have both tunes and need to choose which to listen to. We can shape our lives around the disappointment and meaninglessness of this age, or we can shape our lives around the love of Christ in us.

## BUILDING WITH GOLD EACH DAY

This is a purpose that can get you up in the morning and that can transform the disappointments of a humdrum, repetitive job, relationship or life. You can always love the person you are interacting with. You can always get off the couch and go find a way to love someone else. You can always build with gold.

And then you can enjoy the box set, movie night or computer game without loading on it a weight of meaning that it can never carry. The game can stay as just a game. It's not the point.

Loving those around us as God loves us doesn't remove the disappointments from life; but it stops them from forcing us to escape. We can live in this world of disappointment, not with sad resignation, but with real purpose. With the Spirit's help, we can love our family, friends and colleagues and even strangers right now, today, as we go about our normal business. You can put down this book and live out the purpose for which God made you. You are loved by God, and you can love the person in front of you, whoever that may be. You are reading this book in the middle of a disappointing life and you are reading this book in the middle of a life filled with purpose.

The star-fighter won't come in reality. But don't be disappointed about that. You never needed it to. You have a greater and more exciting purpose—one that is real.

# 6. PERSPECTIVE THAT SHRINKS DISAPPOINTMENT

A week ago I sat with an elderly friend in a nursing home. She passed away two days later. When I was with her, she couldn't speak much, so I talked, read the Bible to her and prayed. I hope my friend was blessed by what we read. I certainly was, as I read aloud parts of the Bible that talked about the coming day of Christ's return. I was glad to gain perspective on my life now—on life lived in the shadow of death, but where perspective does not come from seeing the misery of death but from the coming of life.

## CHRIST IS COMING BACK

> Now, brothers and sisters, about times and dates we do not need to write to you, for you know very well that the day of the Lord will come like a thief in the night. While people are saying, "Peace and safety", destruction will come on them suddenly, as labour pains on a pregnant woman, and they will not escape. (1 Thessalonians 5 v 1-3)

The day of the Lord will come like a thief. The point is the surprise, not the result—Christ will not come to take, but to give. But it will be without warning. The thief doesn't send you an email to let you know the date when he will burgle your house, and then send you a one-hour thievery window when he will be with you. Similarly, labour pains come on a woman unannounced; but they are not unexpected. As a pregnant woman nears the time of delivery, she doesn't know the hour, but she knows that the hour will come.

As you have been reading this book, you will have been dwelling on some of the disappointments in your life, and in the lives of your family, church family and friends. Perhaps you have been trying to magnify Christ and put these disappointments into perspective. Wonderfully, as we do this, we can remember that there will come a day when we do not need to remember to magnify Christ—when right perspective will be as obvious as the view from a mountain's summit.

In this life, seeing Jesus clearly—making him as big in our sight as he is in reality—is hard. One day, it will be natural:

> For now we see only a reflection as in a mirror; then we shall see face to face. Now I know in part; then I shall know fully, even as I am fully known.
>
> (1 Corinthians 13 v 12)

When Christ returns, we will not need to remind ourselves of his love because the strength of his embrace and the warmth of his smile will leave no doubt.

And we simply do not know when this will be. It may be that this will be the last sentence you read before Christ leaps from his throne and dives through the heavens with the speed and joy of a husband returning for his bride after a long time away. And if you are now reading still, I am sorry that it is not yet the appointed hour (I was a bit disappointed to finish writing these words), but Christ will return.

This life is fleeting. The man who wrote these words to the Thessalonian and Corinthian churches knew terrible suffering, injustices and, perhaps worst of all, the disappointment of churches falling apart and fellow-workers for the gospel abandoning the cause. Yet Paul sums up these sufferings and disappointments as "light and momentary troubles" (2 Corinthians 4 v 17). They are not light and momentary in themselves—Paul bore heavy burdens, and shouldered them for years and years—but they became so as he compared them to the "eternal glory that far outweighs them all". When we are able to see life with the perspective of eternity, the perspective of Christ's glorious return, our troubles become only light and relatively momentary. So yes, as we have seen, we have hope and purpose for today; but today is not what we are living for. We must always be longing for and looking for a better world. We were not made for this disappointing life, but for one full of satisfaction in Christ.

We need to remember this in the normal course of life. It is hard—there have been two thousand years of disappointment since Christ left, and you have lived however long and not yet known a single day in the bodily presence of Jesus. But this simply means that we are now far closer to the day of Christ's return than we were. You are a day closer to infinitely long, glorious and satisfied life than you were yesterday. Jesus is coming back. You will see him face to face. You will! One day, maybe soon, Jesus is coming back.


## JUDGMENT DAY AND THE ADOPTION COURT

We saw in chapter 4 how the judgment of Christ is a blessing to us. It re-establishes meaning in a world that seems meaningless.

It brings with it the promise of vindication and resurrection life that are the gifts of Christ to us. And it transforms both us and the creation. We will be adopted as children of God:

> We ourselves, who have the firstfruits of the Spirit, groan
> inwardly as we wait eagerly for our adoption to sonship,
> the redemption of our bodies. (Romans 8 v 23)

Like many of the promises of God, adoption has a present and future dimension. We have been adopted as God's children (Romans 8 v 15), and we will be adopted as his children (v 23).

Imagine a lonely child in an orphanage who has never known what it is to be part of a loving family, who gets the wonderful news that she has been adopted. She can scarcely believe it, and so one of the staff gives her a copy of the paperwork proving it. She memorises the names of her new parents from the document, and then is overjoyed to receive a letter from them. They live a long distance away, but they will, they promise, come to get her.

Suddenly the normal disappointments with life—a meal she doesn't like, friends in the orphanage being mean—seem like small things. It won't be long until her new mum is cooking her dinner! Loneliness isn't loneliness when you know that you're loved. Even the huge and brutal disappointment of her broken family life, which ended up with her sitting in a social worker's office and now on an orphanage bed, is put into perspective. The story won't end here—there is a new chapter, and a new home. Every day she wonders if it will be today. Every night she knows it's a day closer and prays it will be tomorrow. And then, after a couple of weeks that stretch out like decades, there is a knock on her dormitory door and in come a man and a woman whose smiles are nearly as wide as hers.

This is our story—although its beginning is more bleak.

The orphanage we are in is more like a workhouse from a Charles Dickens novel. If life in the workhouse is all that there is, then disappointments are many, satisfaction is rare and hope is gone. But once we know that we are adopted, and that our great Father is coming for us, then our disappointments fade in the new perspective produced by this fact. Indeed, the greatest disappointment becomes simply that we're not with him yet. But we will be. We have our papers. Christ has signed them, and the Spirit has sealed them. What a day it will be when our Father throws open that door!

We are adopted, and we will be adopted. We are children of God. That is not just a phrase. No, it is as real and close as saying I am a child of Tim Hindley. Indeed, even more real and even closer. We are children of the One who is love. We are children of the Father of Jesus Christ, who loves us in the same way that he loves his eternal Son. Our disappointments now are put into perspective; they dim in comparison with the light that is flooding through the already-opening door of our workhouse dormitory.

We have a new family. And we have a new home. Listen again to Paul in Romans 8:

> For the creation was subjected to frustration, not by its own choice, but by the will of the one who subjected it, in hope that the creation itself will be liberated from its bondage to decay and brought into the freedom and glory of the children of God. We know that the whole creation has been groaning as in the pains of childbirth right up to the present time. (v 20-22)

On the day when we are adopted, the creation will be renewed. It will be liberated and "brought into the freedom and glory of the children of God". The renewal of creation is connected with our freedom. The close connection suggests that this is not simply that the two coincide, but that as Christ frees us, so we, with him, free creation. On the new earth, Christ will end and undo disappointment, and we will do it with him.

The creation is waiting for the day when it will be set free. We immediately think that this will be done by God, as he remakes the world as he had made it to be in the beginning. And it will be, but that is not what Paul stresses. He connects the recreation of the world, the end of the frustration, decay and disappointment, with the "freedom and glory of the children of God". There is a parallel between the groaning of creation as it awaits liberation and our groaning as we await adoption as sons of God. As the light floods in, it is not just that the children are adopted, but that the children get to help to totally transform the drab and dirty workhouse dormitory into a palace fit for children of a heavenly King, and for the King himself. It will be as good as new, because it will be totally renewed.

Waiting in the orphanage, it would be a joy to close your eyes and imagine what your new home will be like. As you wait for your new mum and dad, you fill in the background by thinking of your new room and the new garden you'll get to enjoy. It is the parents you long for, but the place will be where you live out the new relationships. Our Father has adopted us, and the great work of renewing the creation will be done by his Son. But when he first made the world, Adam was to keep it, serve it and fill it. When the Lord gave Old Testament Israel a land, they had to move in, build, plant and harvest. We will be given a new home, and Christ will show us to our room. He will also help us to paint it and set it out as we please. We will be creative, working alongside our creative Father. Just as the new creation will show his artistry and imagination at their most beautiful, he will give us ample opportunity to express our own redeemed imaginations.

As you wait in the orphanage, it is a lot easier to bear with the damp patch on one wall of your room, the flaking paint or the nasty colour scheme when you imagine your new home. We do not only have our imaginations—our Father has sent us plenty of descriptions, and set the old, broken, fallen creation before us. He invites us to wonder what it will be like. He invites us to set our disappointments with the world now within the perspective of a new home as well as a new relationship.

## LEFT BEHIND AND UNDONE

When Christ returns, some disappointments will simply fade away to nothing. Maybe you were disappointed never to get the job you had hoped for, or to end your career somewhere in the middle ranks when you had dreamed of being a manager, partner, CEO or whatever. Maybe you have never had the chance to work, prevented by illness, lack of education or simply because you were given no opportunity to do that. As Christ appoints you to work in his new creation, this disappointment will be forgotten as you revel in work that completely suits your character, ability and dreams. It's as if he knows exactly what you hoped for!

But some things cannot fade so easily. Perhaps the deepest and most desperate disappointments are caused by the people who let us down, or who we let down. How will these fade? The answer is that Christ will do more here than simply outshine them.

Take divorce, which is almost always a terrible disappointment for those involved. Each situation is different, but I have not known a divorce that did not cause deep pain to both husband and wife, whatever the causes. In some ways, these disappointments will dim in the light of our marriage to Christ as part of the bride, his church. But relationships and people are eternal, and Christ has something better for the divorced couple than only a better marriage to himself. Imagine catching sight of the person who brought the bitter disappointment of divorce into your life, now righteous and perfect in Christ, as you are. Imagine understanding what actually happened, seeing the lies of Satan for what they were, seeing your sin and theirs laid bare and yet forgiven and removed. The conversation will not be awkward. There will be a chance to joyfully undo the disappointment. It will not be a painful probing or an open wound, but a gentle balm to soften any scars.

Or maybe you were involved in a nasty church split that hurt you, or people you care for. As you sit down and pour a glass with the elder who ripped your church in half, you will be able to laugh with him at how silly at least one of you was (and possibly both of you were) to hold so tightly to something other than Christ. You will swap stories and realise that the kingdom was not hindered—it was always in the hands of a good King.

You may well have disappointments in your life that are harder to work out than that. I do not know how the conversations will go between people who stood on different sides of shield walls, trench-lines, picket lines or courtrooms. It is hard to conceive of them even starting between guards and victims from concentration camps, or slaves and traffickers. We simply don't know how Christ, and the Spirit working in us, will undo these disappointments through his people, in his people. But he will. The promise is that every tear will be wiped away—that there will be a new order of things with no more mourning or pain.

The judgment of Christ is not simply a judgment of people. It is far wider. In Revelation 20 v 14, John sees death and Hades thrown into the lake of fire. The sources of decay, evil, frustration and pain are themselves destroyed. Christ's judgment is a judgment on all evil, on all frustration, on all disappointment. So there will be none left in his new creation. There will be no disappointment that is beyond his power to undo, to redeem. And he will use us to undo and redeem them. They will fade, or they will be filled with new light as we unpack together what Christ has done through, in and despite our disappointments.

This is the perspective you can have as we look at today's disappointments. They are nowhere near as big, permanent or defining as they seem, however sad and wrong they are. Compared to the glory of eternity they really are, though painful and perhaps permanent in this life, light and momentary.

## CHRIST WILL RULE (WHICH IS WONDERFUL)

The real world is the one that is coming. This is the world that is passing:

> So we fix our eyes not on what is seen, but on what is unseen, since what is seen is temporary, but what is unseen is eternal. (2 Corinthians 4 v 18)

Doing this takes practice. Read the Bible with eyes deliberately open to see the world to come. There are wonderful passages that describe it (start with Revelation 21 – 22 and Isaiah 65, for example), and there are far more that give pictures of the hope we have—whether it is in the Jerusalem of Solomon (see 2 Chronicles 9 v 13-28), or the life of Jesus (John 2 v 1-17, for example) or in countless other places (you could start with Psalms, like 23 and 133; Song of Songs 4; Isaiah 32 v 1-8; or Ezekiel 47). The new world is always breaking through. It lurks in the goodness that is left in this creation, and it leaps in with the work of the Lord in the lives of his people. (One book that will help you in this is *Eternity Changes Everything* by Stephen

Witmer, which was a huge blessing to me by fixing my thoughts more often and more firmly on the new creation.)

Next, take time to imagine. Maybe you struggle to see how particular disappointments will be undone. Maybe you struggle to imagine life without the emptiness you feel each day. Well then, struggle! Keep thinking; keep struggling to see how it can be good. It will be good; you know the answer, and the answer lies in Christ, so show your working. And do this with friends. Lay out your disappointments before your brothers and sisters at church and invite them to have a go at guessing what Jesus will do to redeem, mend and glorify himself in these situations.

We have seen that in the good news of Christ we find hope, purpose and perspective. The resurrection gives us hope that death and disappointment are not the end. This hope gives us simple, satisfying and delightful purpose in our lives— the purpose of loving others as we have been loved, as Christ himself loves. And so we can see our disappointment now from the perspective of an eternal, perfectly satisfied life, because the workhouse door is unlocked and one day—maybe today—Christ will fling it open.

Now you have the chance to make this real. The next few chapters will address some of the areas of disappointment in our lives, and apply what we have been seeing to those situations. But before you turn the page to start on that section of this book, take some time, grab a pen and paper, and identify some specific disappointments in your life. How do the hope, purpose and perspective that Christ gives us connect with these disappointments? How do they undo some of the power of those disappointments over you?

You never know... Christ may come back as you scribble. He really might.

# 7. DISAPPOINTED WITH... MY SITUATION

Stuart arrives at his church midweek Bible study group weary. It is not so much that the day's work has been particularly hard; it is just that he is bored and despondent. It all seems so pointless, and so endless.

Ruth isn't even thinking about the group as she knocks on the door shortly after her husband. She is tired and frazzled, sure she's forgotten something and aware that there is a load of washing that needs to go on when she gets home.

When the group leader asks them to turn to Philippians 4, both Stuart and Ruth feel perplexed, and a little guilty, but also hopeful when he reads. Maybe, they think, this could really be possible for Christians today:

> I know what it is to be in need, and I know what it is to have plenty. I have learned the secret of being content in any and every situation, whether well fed or hungry, whether living in plenty or in want. I can do all this through him who gives me strength. (Philippians 4 v 12-13)

Paul describes finding contentment as discovering a secret. It is not a secret like a mystery or a puzzle; it is no riddle, nor is it hidden behind doors and locks. It is a secret hidden in plain sight—the truth that he can do everything through Christ, who strengthens him.

The answer to our over-disappointment with things that are wrong or lacking in our lives, and to living joyfully with our right disappointment is not rocket science—it is Christ's love for us. That's the answer to disappointment because it is the hope, purpose and perspective that the death, resurrection, reign and inevitable return of Jesus give us.

But we still need to learn the "secret", because these truths need living out in the very ordinary mess of life. Doing this is not instinctive. We need to be instructed. We need to learn how to find joy in, through and despite our disappointment.


**WORK AND FAMILY**

Let's consider the two couple we just met: Stuart and Ruth.

*The disappointment of Stuart's work.* Stuart is sitting at his desk on Tuesday afternoon, willing the hands on the clock to move faster. He has no more clients today, and needs to reply to some emails and do some work on the mortgage applications he went through with people earlier in the day. There's some online training he could get on with. Or not.

He has done fairly well. Most of his friends are still stuck in the jobs they had when they left school or university. At least at the bank he's progressed from behind the counter to sitting out in the banking hall and dealing with mortgages and loans.

A couple of his friends have gone far, and he still feels a bit jealous every time Christine is over from head office. Especially as he used to do better than her in maths! He knows this isn't the end of the road, but he can see that his career trajectory will probably end upstairs as a junior manager, rather than in the head office.

How does Stuart learn to be content when his dreams of satisfying work seem almost out of reach? How does he magnify Christ in this situation? The beginning of the answer is always to realise that Jesus is alive, and that he is coming back. Stuart's career trajectory will not end upstairs at an assistant manager's desk. It will end on a throne, sharing the rule of Christ over the cosmos. This work is temporary. It is not what it was meant to be (and neither would it be if he did have Christine's job). It is thorns and thistles, frustrating and burdensome, and fleeting.

But that reality does not mean that Stuart simply sits back and wills the clock to go faster until the end of the age rather than the end of the day. His work has purpose, because Christ is ruling now. The purpose of his job is not to achieve great things, if "great things" means making it to director, or making himself a fortune. The purpose of his job is to display the love of God to the world. He has ample opportunities to do this, if he'd only look, and there is deep joy in pursuing it, despite the frustrations of work in this world. By working hard this afternoon on the mortgage applications, he can love his customers well. By engaging with the training, he can serve future customers and his employer better. By seeing the emails as communication from real people, he can work out how to respond to them in the way that makes their life easiest. Rather than simply batting the problem to someone else, and just cc'ing the original sender, he can do some work to respond fully. He can take work off his colleagues and onto himself. He can go an extra mile.

As he does so, he can pray for the chance to explain why he is working like this. He can serve the cause of Christ by praying for opportunities to share the good news with his colleagues. Then he might know the joy of leading someone to Christ, as well as the joy of working in love.

Stuart is made up (you knew that), but this reality is not. At the church I was part of in Manchester, we ran a number of courses for people who wanted to find out more about Christianity. Regularly colleagues of my wife came on these courses. The way Flick went about her work as an accountant was striking to them. I think they found it particularly striking that she worked hard, and was prepared to go the extra mile when needed, but she was also committed to leaving on time when she was meeting with people to read the Bible, or had church family round for supper. The example of someone working hard, but at the same time having a God who mattered more than work, was intriguing, and made people interested to find out just what sort of Lord motivated her. To work "as working for the Lord, not for human masters" (Colossians 3 v 23) is noticeable when you live that way day in, day out.

None of this means that the Stuarts in their offices around the world won't find their work disappointing. But it does mean that you, if you see any of your situation in Stuart's, can know deep and joyful purpose in the midst of disappointment. You can look forward to the smile on the face, the slap on the back and the "well done, good and faithful servant" when you next see your Boss (Matthew 25 v 21). And just maybe there will be an office reunion in the new creation, as your colleagues gather together to talk about old times and to thank you for sharing the gospel with them.

*The disappointment of Ruth's children.* Ruth is on parental leave with her four-month old baby, and also looking after a three-year old when he's not at pre-school. She loves her children, and would react strongly if you asked whether they were a disappointment to her. They really aren't.

Life is not what she had expected, though. There are some lovely times where Harry plays with his little brother, some sunny trips to the park, some good coffees with other mums.

The problem is that there is just so much washing. So much washing, cleaning, wiping the floor under the high chair, shopping with a screaming baby. There are so many nappies, short nights, trips to the doctor, expensive shoes. And she is always exhausted. Ruth has to work out soon whether to go back to work, and can't decide which is worse—the thought of handling all this and her job, or the thought of never escaping the washing line.

The hope, purpose and perspective of Jesus impact Ruth slightly differently to Stuart. She doesn't need to be told to count her blessings. She prayed for children, and she has friends at church suffering with infertility. Her children are a source of joy to her. She also sees more easily the purposefulness of raising her children. She knows that she and her husband have a unique opportunity to teach these little ones to know and love the Lord. That does give purpose to her life, but day in, day out there seems a lot more time spent on changing nappies than teaching the gospel.

Here, though, is a picture of the ministry of Christ. A mother, seeking to serve her children well, dies to herself. In embracing the drudgery of chores, the endless need to discipline and instruct children, the loss of tidiness, order, space, leisure and sleep for the sake of love, she mirrors Christ's sacrifice for her. If she lets it, the gospel can change Ruth's perspective to show her that she is taking up her cross daily in imitation of her Lord. As she sees the glory of this frustrating ministry, she can rejoice in the frustrations—the disappointment is drawing her more closely to Christ.

## PEOPLE LET US DOWN

The reality of disappointment is that it is often caused by people. Sometimes this is the general current of the world we live in. As our friends use social media to showcase a sanitised, satisfied, funny and fulfilled version of their lives, we feel more disappointed. As the TV shows give us glamour, sophistication and romance, we are more disappointed at the lack of these in normal life.

People are the greatest source of disappointment to us. When Adam saw his bride, he sang with delight over her: "This is now bone of my bones and flesh of my flesh" (Genesis 2 v 23). Here at last was a companion for him—a wife he could delight in. Men and women have sung about love, compatibility, romance and marriage ever since.

But the truth is that you do not live in Eden, and so your marriage does not match up to what Adam and Eve enjoyed. And the truth is that Hollywood makes fictional films, so your marriage does not match up to a cinematic "happily ever after". If you are married, then it would be surprising if your husband or wife was not a disappointment. It would also be surprising if you did not feel the shame and remorse of knowing that you are a disappointment to them.

Let's imagine Stuart and Ruth's life a bit further down the line. Nothing is spectacularly wrong, but they are both living with disappointment. Stuart has just been turned down for a promotion to assistant manager and is feeling angry that Ruth is so clearly disappointed. He fears she is more disappointed in him than for him. He fears she might be right to feel that. He feels as if he works his socks off for the family, at the bank and at home, but that Ruth never seems to notice.

Ruth has gone back to teaching part-time at the school where her son is, and wishes she didn't know what she does. Harry is in trouble at school, often, and she has seen from other, older students she has taught the trajectory that he is on. This is worrying, but perhaps most disappointing is that neither of their sons shares her love of learning, especially of reading. She doesn't care if they are successful, but she can't work out how to connect with them. It is fine for Stuart, who plays computer games with them, but she feels excluded from her own family.

I am guessing that you are disappointed with someone. Your parents have let you down. Your children have. Your friends have. Your church have. Your pastor has. Maybe in little ways, maybe in terrible ones, maybe somewhere in between. Perhaps you were being unrealistic. But very possibly you were not. They just fell short—far short—of what you had every right to expect of them.

In this disappointment, we need to remember that sin really is real. We need to learn not to be surprised by sin.

Sin is shocking. I find it disturbing how mean I can be to my wife. I am scared how angry I get with my children. Sometimes the harsh, cynical ways I talk about my friends make me angry (with myself, but perversely I often blame them for that too). Sin is shocking, and it is shockingly common. So common that we will be terribly disappointed by some of those who should stand by us. The friend who should have our back might well stab us in it. The husband we promised to love for better or for worse is most likely to be the cause of the "worse". We will tell our children that we love them through gritted teeth. Sin should always be shocking, but we need to stop letting it be surprising.

When we forget that others are sinful, we over-react in disappointment at their sin. We get angry, we withdraw, we stop trusting. The end of this road is emotional shutdown and relational isolation. People will disappoint you. And if you are surprised by sin and so push them away, you will end up with no one to love, and no one to love you.

We must not be surprised by sin. And we must not forget the power of the Holy Spirit. There is a Saviour who has wrestled hope from despair, life from death, light from darkness. Jesus can redeem anyone, and any relationship. Sin is very common, but the Holy Spirit is very, very powerful. We must not be surprised by sin, but equally we do not have to be resigned to it. We can be hopeful when faced with people who disappoint us. We can be prayerful. God is greater than any situation and any sin. Prodigal children do return. Marriages fractured by unfaithfulness can be mended. Distant parents can grow warm. Things can be changed. Not by us, no—but by him.

So who do you find disappointing? Who has let you down badly? It would surprise me if your closest family were not on that list in some ways; and there's no need to feel bad about acknowledging that (you are probably on their lists too). How do you restore joyful love to these relationships scarred by past hurts and present disappointment? Hopefully the joy that comes from hope, purpose and perspective will go some way towards that. Your hope was never in that relationship, but in Christ. Assuming it does not place you in danger, you can offer love within that relationship, just like Christ. And one day you will enjoy only perfect relationships, in the presence of Christ.

And you can pray. Without the Spirit, you will either strive fruitlessly to change the situations you're disappointed with or the people you're disappointed in, or you'll despair of them. But the Spirit can grow fruit and bring hope. He may do it through you, or around you. So pray. Let your disappointments be fuel for firing your prayers, and not the burden that dampens your love.

We pray so little, as though it achieved so little. What fools we are, for there is nothing like the power, love and wisdom of the Creator of all things. When such a mighty King is our Father, why would we not ask? Pray now.

# 8. DISAPPOINTED WITH...
## MY SUCCESS

Yesterday evening, I undertook a dangerous activity. I mowed the lawn.

This is not normally considered an extreme sport, but it holds great danger for me at the moment; not because I have a mower liable to explode, or a garden with an enormous crevice in it, but because I have laid some new turf. I am very satisfied with the new turf. It is verdant and lush, and makes the whole house look better. And that's why it is dangerous, because I am one of those middle-aged men who is tempted to worship his house, especially the parts that look better as a result of the work of his hands.

I remember as a young man wondering why so many people in my church were always doing up their houses. Most of the guys over thirty seemed to spend the weekends laying decking, painting walls and wasting hours in DIY shops. 20-year-old me just didn't get it—their houses were nicer than my flat before they began to do anything, and I was doing nothing more creative than putting the odd poster up. Now I've joined the DIY club—and I wonder why younger people don't do something more productive with their weekends...

Of course there is nothing wrong with laying turf or enjoying doing up your house. But for me it really is a dangerous temptation to find my sense of satisfaction in my DIY (or my sense of disappointment—witness the great trampoline-measuring failure back in chapter 3). And so mowing the lawn last night was a dangerous activity... until I finished. Then, tired, I lay on my back on top of our picnic table and looked at the sky. As I did, I was struck by its vastness, and then by the greatness of the God who made it. Suddenly, by the kind work of the Spirit, I was drawn to repent of my lawn-worshipping idolatry (yes, that's what it is) and enjoy the wonder of Christ. With such a perspective, my new lawn was transformed from a god to a gift. I could enjoy the new lawn as a tiny reflection of the Lord who laid all the grass on the face of the earth and enjoyed it, declaring it good. I could enjoy the lawn as a gift from Christ and give thanks to him for it.

We saw back in chapter 3 how disappointing success can be. Now we are going to see how to turn away from our disappointment with the successes in our lives. We're going to apply the great truths of chapters 4 – 6 in reverse: how does a new perspective, a greater purpose and an unshakeable hope shake us free from the disappointment of success.

You might remember Paul and Anna, the imaginary teacher and nurse we considered in chapter 3. Their disappointment was rooted in the failure of their successful lives to deliver the satisfaction they had expected. Maybe you see some of them in the mirror. You have the career, house, marriage, children, or whatever it was that you hoped for when you were starting out on life. Maybe you have more than you dreamed of. And maybe you have found that there is still a gnawing sense of disappointment—that unspoken feeling or fear that there must be more to life than this. If this is you, then you are at an important junction in your life. To see that the purposes you live for and the success you crave do not satisfy is a God-gifted opportunity to you—and offers you the opportunity to find true, lasting satisfaction, purpose and hope. It might sound strange to consider dissatisfaction a blessing. But your dissatisfaction can lead you to search for, and find, someone truly satisfying.

Remember the secret to contentment that Paul had found?

> I know what it is to be in need, and I know what it is to have plenty. I have learned the secret of being content in any and every situation, whether well fed or hungry, whether living in plenty or in want. I can do all this through him who gives me strength.
>
> (Philippians 4 v 12-13)

Paul had found the secret of joyful contentment when things were hard—and when he was "living in plenty". In other words, contentment needs learning when things are good. When all is right with the world, we still need to learn how to find true joy and lasting satisfaction in Christ, rather than in our pleasant circumstances.


## THE FOOLISH WEALTHY MAN

Christ is coming back to judge the world. How will he judge our successful lives, and how can we live in the light of that judgment now? This is foundational if we are to live in ways that others would see as successful without seeking to find our satisfaction in this success. When we do find our primary satisfaction in a successful career, family, house or whatever, we become idolaters, worshipping a false god called "Wife" or

"Sales figures" or "Lawn". Since those cisterns are cracked, we must become disappointed idolaters, worshiping a god that will never be able to deliver the satisfaction it promises.

One of Jesus' most sobering parables was about a man who enjoyed great success:

> Someone in the crowd said to [Jesus], "Teacher, tell my brother to divide the inheritance with me."
>
> Jesus replied, "Man, who appointed me a judge or an arbiter between you?" Then he said to them, "Watch out! Be on your guard against all kinds of greed; life does not consist in an abundance of possessions."
>
> And he told them this parable: "The ground of a certain rich man yielded an abundant harvest. He thought to himself, 'What shall I do? I have no place to store my crops.'
>
> "Then he said, 'This is what I'll do. I will tear down my barns and build bigger ones, and there I will store my surplus grain. And I'll say to myself, "You have plenty of grain laid up for many years. Take life easy; eat, drink and be merry."'
>
> "But God said to him, 'You fool! This very night your life will be demanded from you. Then who will get what you have prepared for yourself?'
>
> "This is how it will be with whoever stores up things for themselves but is not rich towards God."
>
> (Luke 12 v 13-21)

By drawing judgment into the imminent future for this man, Jesus shows very simply how foolish it is to live for wealth. Any assessment of our security, status or satisfaction based on the things we have now and not based on God's opinion of us at the day of judgment is dangerously short-sighted. Your reputation among your colleagues doesn't matter much if God is going to say to you, "You fool".

Christ is not teaching anything new here. He is simply applying the teaching of Ecclesiastes. Solomon knew well the emptiness of success: "Whoever loves money never has enough; whoever loves wealth is never satisfied with their income. This too is meaningless" (Ecclesiastes 5 v 10). The technique Solomon uses to expose the disappointment of success is exactly the same as Jesus—he takes us to the verdict of judgment day. "Everyone comes naked from their mother's womb, and as everyone comes, so they depart" (Ecclesiastes 5 v 15).

As we have seen, though, he says this as a goad. The warning that the judgment of Christ will lay bare the emptiness of every false god we build and cling to is a goad to prod us into repentance. So how do we repent of the sin of seeking satisfaction in our success?

Christ spares us devastating loss on the day of judgment and he spares us desperate disappointment now by showing us his glory. It is as we see his greatness and his ability to satisfy our deepest desires that we find it easy to see the silliness of the gods of worldly success. If you see Christ truly, you want to grasp him with both hands, and you hardly notice that you have let go of your dreams of success to do so.

## THE DISAPPOINTED WEALTHY MAN

In terms of wealth, Zacchaeus was a success. In his career, he was a success—a chief tax collector. The money and status had cost him—his Jewish community hated tax collectors, who worked for the occupying Romans. He must have valued money very highly to be prepared to take on the hatred of his town for the sake of wealth.

By the time we meet him, it seems that Zacchaeus was disappointed with his wealth. His money had bought him only that sense that there must be something else. This would have been a tragedy if he had not reacted as he did; but because he was prepared to climb a tree to get a glimpse of an itinerant preacher who had no money at all, his disappointment proved to be a mercy. We don't know what he expected from seeing Jesus, and perhaps he didn't know himself. He had a yearning for more—for a joy that his wealth had promised and then failed to deliver.

And he found the more he was after:

> When Jesus reached the spot, he looked up and said to him, "Zacchaeus, come down immediately. I must stay at your house today." So he came down at once and welcomed him gladly.
>
> All the people saw this and began to mutter, "He has gone to be the guest of a sinner."
>
> But Zacchaeus stood up and said to the Lord, "Look, Lord! Here and now I give half of my possessions to the poor, and if I have cheated anybody out of anything, I will pay back four times the amount."
>
> Jesus said to him, "Today salvation has come to this house, because this man, too, is a son of Abraham. For the Son of Man came to seek and to save the lost."
>
> (Luke 19 v 5-10)

By his kindness to Zacchaeus, Jesus shifted his perspective. There was no way that Zacchaeus deserved to have the Son of God come under his roof. He was a sinner, and Jesus knew this. That is why he came for him. By accepting him, welcoming him and even putting himself in the humble position of receiving Zacchaeus' hospitality, Jesus subjected Zacchaeus to the kindest judgment. Seeing Christ up close, Zacchaeus wanted to be his. He wanted Jesus and so he was saved—saved out of his disappointing success.

And so he lets go of his success. Half his possessions go to the poor. With the rest, he pays back four times over those he's cheated. No half measures here. The closed fist is now an open palm. In taking hold of Christ, Zacchaeus has hardly noticed that he has let go of the money he clung to so desperately before.

Can you see what Zacchaeus saw? Salvation is freedom. It is the freedom to repent. Repentance is not the gritted-teeth effort to let go of a sin we cherish. It is gladly reaching out to take hold of Christ. It is to let go of what, as our god, could brings us only disappointment us as we worshipped it, and to come to the God who will bring us only satisfaction us as we worship him.

## THE TRUE MEASURE OF SUCCESS

Salvation transforms success. It changes our view of what success is. This is hinted at in the Zacchaeus episode and written clearly all over the Bible. Success for him had been piling the money up on the table. Success for him became welcoming Jesus at his table and loving others with his money. He had a new purpose. So do we.

The writer to the Hebrews reminds his readers of the days after their salvation, when:

> You suffered along with those in prison and joyfully
> accepted the confiscation of your property, because

you knew that you yourselves had better and lasting possessions. (Hebrews 10 v 34)

These Christians were able to joyfully see their wealth, homes and businesses taken from them. They were able not just to endure this suffering but to rejoice in it, because they understood the coming judgment day. Their property would not endure, but their heavenly treasure would. They were heavily invested in Christ and his gospel cause. This freed them to love. They loved those in prison even at the cost of their houses. The cost of visiting, caring for and siding with Christians who had been arrested was high. But they paid it. They saw that true success lay not in an abundance of possessions but in an abundance of love.

There are two sorts of success. There is the success that this world offers—wealth, power, status, authority, respect, fame, or whatever. These will mean little or nothing, or worse, on judgment day when this world is rolled up. Then there is the success that Christ defines. Real success is to love as we are loved: to know the joy of being Christ's and being like Christ.

On the day of Christ's coming, it will be this real success that is measured. It will be our loves that shine—our love for him, our love for his people that caused us to care for them well, and our love for the lost that drove us to speak the gospel to them.

When we hear a politician resign to "spend more time with my family", we smile cynically. The idea of an important person giving up their status and salary to love their family more is laughable to us.

It is not laughable to Christ. It makes perfect sense to the Son of God who left the position of supreme authority for the death of a slave. It makes perfect sense to the One who left the throne of light for a wooden manger and a wooden cross for the sake of his bride. Jesus Christ measures success by different standards to political commentators or newspaper readers.

In the kingdom of heaven there is a reversal. "The last will be first, and the first will be last" (Matthew 20 v 16). So seek real success; seek it by taking up your cross; seek it by giving yourself to love your enemy and pray for those who persecute you. Seek success by all means, according to the criteria of the day of the Lord. Seek success that will be judged as success by Jesus. It is freeing and satisfying.

## THE TRUE ROUTE TO REAL SUCCESS

To do this in practice, in the grit and grime of normal daily life, we look beyond today. We were made to see Christ. We were created for life with him, sinless and pure. When he returns, he will remove our dross and we will be pure gold before him. He has begun that process now.

The fuel for living a truly successful life is to know that you will one day live it perfectly, and with perfect satisfaction. Yesterday you did not live a life of perfect love, but tomorrow you might, if Christ returns today. When he comes, every tomorrow into all eternity you will live a perfectly loving life just as he does. Truly satisfying success is not a pipe dream— it is inevitable for those who follow Jesus.

So redefine your view of success. Review those things you look to for satisfaction—particularly if you have them. Received with thankfulness, a good job, marriage, house, family, car or whatever is a blessing and a joy. It only becomes a disappointment when you think it should mark final, ultimate, complete success. It doesn't, and it will never satisfy you. But Jesus will, and Jesus does.

Think through where the world would see you as successful. If that success was the best it ever got for you, how would it fail to be truly and eternally satisfying and joyful? Now consider how that same blessing can be a hint of the glory that is coming when Christ returns. How does worshipping Jesus enable you to enjoy your worldly success without worshipping it or worrying about losing it? How does he promise something of a similar sort or type, but of far greater significance or permanence? If your worldly success is your greatest success, you are in for a life of disappointment. If it becomes a reminder of where you find your true satisfaction, and what real success is now and right through into eternity, you are in for a life of joy.

I must remember that next time I mow the lawn. When must you?

# 9. DISAPPOINTED WITH... MY MINISTRY

Two years into pastoring a new church plant, I was deeply disappointed about it.

I am the pastor of Broadgrace, a small church in rural North Norfolk, England. Broadgrace was planted in 2010, and by the end of 2012 I did not know if we had done the right thing. We had seen very little numerical growth, and I was worried that we might have seen just as little spiritual growth. I certainly felt that my faith was small and dwindling. Sunday meetings felt like hard work.

I don't want to overplay it, I loved being part of the church and was always grateful for the brothers and sisters the Lord had brought us together with. I depended on them to show me Christ, and still do. I began to question, though, what the Lord had brought me to Norfolk for. Had I simply been wrong to think that he had called us to start a church in this part of the world? Or were we getting something wrong? Were we being unfaithful in some significant area? Or had the Lord given us a ministry of judgment, to be holding out the gospel to people who would not listen. As I mulled these things over, a particular verse from the Bible buzzed around me like a wasp:

> Who dares despise the day of small things, since the seven eyes of the LORD that range throughout the earth will rejoice when they see the chosen capstone in the hand of Zerubbabel? (Zechariah 4 v 10)

The translation above carries one sense of the original Hebrew words that the Holy Spirit inspired Zechariah to write. It is hard to translate exactly, though, and it can easily carry another sense:

> For whoever has despised the day of small things shall rejoice, and shall see the plumb line in the hand of Zerubbabel. These seven are the eyes of the LORD, which range through the whole earth. (Zechariah 4 v 10, ESV)

I still struggle to know what to make of it. I suspect that it is a deliberately ambiguous verse, with both senses being implied.

It is likely that you are not in full-time Christian work; most Christians aren't. If you are a Christian, though, you have a ministry, or more probably ministries, from the Lord. Some of these might be within your church: maybe you lead a Bible study, or teach a group for young people, or welcome on the door, or do one of the myriad practical tasks that keep churches meeting. Whatever your ministry is, do you feel as though you live in a day of small things? Do you feel that the gospel dynamite that Paul refers to in Romans 1 v 16, where the gospel is "the power of God that brings salvation", simply isn't that powerful? Are you disappointed in the fruit of your ministry?

You should be.

## THE TEARS OF CHRIST

To be disappointed with the results of your ministry is to walk in good company. It is to know something of the heartache of Isaiah and Jeremiah and a host of other prophets. Daniel waited seventy years before he saw Israel return to their land, and even then he knew that it was nothing like the restoration promised. God's true people in the Old Testament "were all commended for their faith, yet none of them received what had been promised" (Hebrews 11 v 39). They all died waiting for satisfaction. In a sense, they all died disappointed—their days were not the days in which the promise was received. But they did not die lacking joy.

Jesus too was disappointed with the response to his ministry:

> As he approached Jerusalem and saw the city, he wept
> over it and said, "If you, even you, had only known on
> this day what would bring you peace – but now it is
> hidden from your eyes." (Luke 19 v 41)

The tears that Christ shed over Jerusalem were tears of disappointment—of frustration that his city would not recognise him and come to him in repentance and faith. Paul knew that disappointment too:

> I speak the truth in Christ—I am not lying, my
> conscience confirms it through the Holy Spirit—I have
> great sorrow and unceasing anguish in my heart. For I
> could wish that I myself were cursed and cut off from
> Christ for the sake of my people, those of my own race,
> the people of Israel. (Romans 9 v 1-4)

So desperate is his disappointment at the lack of response to his preaching of the gospel among the Jewish people that he would trade his own salvation for theirs if he could.

If you are feeling down about your ministry, you are in exalted company. It is a good thing to be disappointed alongside Jesus.

Nevertheless, the same danger of over-disappointment lurks here as elsewhere. For Christ, the indifference and sin of Jerusalem drove him to the cross. For us, it often drives us to self-pity and frustration. We often lose the joy and wonder of serving alongside such a King as Jesus, seeing our ministry but losing sight of the Lord who gifts it to us.

So what is Christ-like disappointment, and what is over-disappointment? A good question to ask yourself is why you are disappointed in your ministry. Are you disappointed primarily for Jesus—that he is being robbed of the worship and glory that he so richly deserves? Are you disappointed also for people—people who are refusing Christ's offer of life and walking away from salvation? Or are you disappointed for yourself? Are you disappointed because the respect, self-worth, success or applause you want deep down have not flowed from your ministry as you hoped. In 2012, two years into our church plant, I think my disappointments were mixed. I was disappointed for Jesus and the people around us, but I was also far too disappointed for myself.

The frightening truth is that it is possible to work hard in your ministry and share Christ clearly and be doing it for all the wrong reasons:

> Some preach Christ out of envy and rivalry, but others out of goodwill. The latter do so out of love, knowing that I am put here for the defence of the gospel. The former preach Christ out of selfish ambition, not sincerely, supposing that they can stir up trouble for me while I am in chains. (Philippians 1 v 15-17)

The message was faithful, but sometimes the motives were selfish ambition and causing trouble for another Christian, Paul. Presumably these preachers wanted to build a reputation for themselves, and to replace Paul as the leader of the mission or steal his reputation within the church. The desire to make a name in ministry, whether among your friends, in your church or across your network of churches, is powerful. It is all too possible for us to be driven by it, and then disappointed because of it. It is certainly an issue for my heart. We know we are not meant to measure success in terms of numbers, but really we do. Numbers are not a very good guide of the success or otherwise of your ministry but they are a very stark one. For you, success might be determined by the numerical success of ministry, or it the good opinion of others.

So think about your ministry, and why you're feeling down about it. Are you disappointed because you think the children in your Sunday school class do not seem to be growing more like Jesus, or are you disappointed because no one seems to even notice the work you put in?

## THE PURPOSE AND SUCCESS CRITERIA FOR MINISTRY

We tend to judge the success of our ministry in terms of measurable outcomes. Numbers are very easy to measure, whether it is numbers in church, or at an event we helped organise, or numbers saved during a course we led. Money is easy to count as well. I am amazed how many people in the church think that the financial viability of an event or ministry is a measure of success—I am far too busy counting the numbers!

We can try to assess spiritual growth as well. If I spend a good deal of time meeting up with a friend whose marriage is in trouble or who is struggling with doubts about Christ, then success is a renewed marriage or strengthened faith. If the future holds divorce or falling away, then I think I have failed. And am I not right to do so? Surely we can judge ministry by such criteria. If I share the gospel and no one is saved, then that must be a failure. Well, not according to Paul:

> You know, brothers and sisters, that our visit to you was not without results. We had previously suffered and been treated outrageously in Philippi, as you know, but with the help of our God we dared to tell you his gospel in the face of strong opposition. For the appeal we make does not spring from error or impure motives, nor are we trying to trick you. On the contrary, we speak as those approved by God to be entrusted with the gospel. We are not trying to please people but God, who tests our hearts. You know we never used flattery, nor did we put on a mask to cover up greed—God is our witness. We were not looking for praise from people, not from you or anyone else, even though as apostles of Christ we could have asserted our authority. Instead, we were like young children among you. Just as a nursing mother cares for her children, so we cared for you. Because we loved you so much, we were delighted to share with you not only the gospel of God but our lives as well.
>
> (1 Thessalonians 2 v 1-8)

Paul's ministry in Thessalonica "was not without results". What were those results? First, he spoke the gospel motivated by a desire to "please ... God, who tests our hearts". Second, he and his team cared for the church, loved them and shared their lives with them. The "results" are the love that Paul showed and the pleasure he brought his God.

There are two liberating ideas here. The first is that the success Christ is looking for from your ministry is faithfulness. To simply speak the truth about Jesus is a successful ministry. Whether the result of ministry is a revival or a riot (as it was in Paul's case—Acts 17 v 1-9) is not in our hands. The Lord looks at what we say, and he is honoured if we are faithful to the gospel. I remember years ago an older Christian advising me that if I saw few saved, I should examine my teaching in case I was being unfaithful; and that if I saw many saved, I should examine my teaching in case I was preaching what people's itching ears wanted to hear.

God wants us to speak the truth faithfully. Of course he cares about who is saved, but that is his responsibility, not ours. The numbers saved in your youth group or at your evangelistic pub quiz are in his remit, not yours. He looks to you for faithfulness, not numbers. His criteria for success are not the same as ours.

So the second liberating idea is that the other factor Christ counts as success in ministry is love. He doesn't want to see my sales figures; he wants to look at my heart. He looks to us to simply love faithfully in the situations he has put us in. He is looking at your ministry and asking: *Do they love those around them so much that they are delighted to share with them not only my gospel, but their lives as well?*

How does this impact your ministry, whether it's in church, in your family, or elsewhere? Do you love the Lord, and those you serve, enough to faithfully speak the gospel to them and share your life with them? Yes? Then that is success, and a defence against the overwhelming disappointment of considering as success factors that Jesus does not, and then becoming crushed or puffed up by them.

## HOPE

First and foremost, I am not a pastor; I am a Christian. Your ministry does not define you and your destiny is not bound up in it. Christ defines you and your life is bound up with his:

> Since, then, you have been raised with Christ, set your hearts on things above, where Christ is, seated at the right hand of God. Set your minds on things above, not on earthly things. For you died, and your life is now hidden with Christ in God. (Colossians 3 v 1-3)

It would be very strange for a wife to find satisfaction in the ways she cared for her husband and looked after him without finding any satisfaction in his love for her. It is just as strange for the bride of Christ, his church, to find satisfaction (or disappointment) in our service of him, and not in his love for us.

There is a paradox here. If we find our life in the great love Christ has for us rather than in the great things we do for him, it means that we will probably not even notice them. When our eyes are on Christ, it seems natural and obvious to pour ourselves out in service of him. A mother who loves her children might be found clearing up, mending and cleaning late into the evening despite a sleepless night with a sick son yesterday and a hectic day at work. She is serving with every fibre of her being, but love makes it natural for her to do so. So too with Christ. Sometimes we fix our eyes on what we wish God had done through us, and so we miss what he has done for us. Often we are so busy being disappointed by what didn't happen in our ministries that we ignore what did happen. And all to easily we forget that our lives are not wrapped up in our service for Christ, but in his resurrection for us.

## PERSPECTIVE

The perspective of the coming judgment of Christ is also a great help in loving others. Will Christ care on the day of judgment whether you completed your ministry "to do" list today? Probably not. Will he care that you ate a cold dinner because you left the table to help a neighbour carry a new table into their house? Yes. Will he be annoyed that you gave money to this missionary and not that ministry? Probably not. Will he be glad that you gave money cheerfully and sacrificially out of love for those who haven't heard the gospel? Absolutely.

The perspective of the judgment day will help us to enjoy loving others, knowing that this will be declared as faithfulness by Jesus on the day he comes. It will help us to neglect many other things that the world, the flesh or the devil tell us are all-important, but that are not all that important from Christ's perspective.

## THE DAY OF SMALL THINGS

Understanding what Jesus calls successful ministry means we can live in the tension of the day of small things. It should be disappointing to live in a day when the gospel does not seem to be going forward in our country. It should be of deep sadness to see such little interest in Christ, such little love for him even in his church, and such little faithfulness even in my heart. We should despise such a day, but not so as to become bitter and not so as to become crushed. The day of small things is still the day in which we can serve Christ. Now is the day of salvation, when we can work in the light. And so we love. We love Jesus, we love his people and we love those lost without him. In doing so our ministry will always be disappointing—we will not see Christ receive the glory he deserves until the day he returns.

Our ministry will also be deeply satisfying, though, because we will follow the pattern of our Lord, who loved us despite our sin and faithlessness.

So Christ-like ministry will be disappointing. And it will be joyful. If you love Jesus and love others then, strangely, your ministry will disappoint you more. You will long for people to be saved, for them to grow, and for Jesus to be honoured. And yet alongside that, your ministry will satisfy you more. You may face a day of tiny things; you may face a riot, as Paul did. But you can please God by sharing a faithful message and sharing a loving life. He is not disappointed with that ministry. Neither should you be.

# 10. DISAPPOINTED WITH...
## MYSELF

I am deeply disappointed with the person I see in the mirror.

While I will often flatter myself, make myself sound good in front of others and excuse myself when I sin, I know underneath it all that I am not the man I wish I was. I am not the husband, father, son or friend I hoped to be. I am so self-absorbed and slow to love and care for those around me. In my mind I have a view of myself as a considerate, compassionate husband. The evidence simply does not support this view. So often when my wife is sad or concerned about something, I am frustrated. I had been hoping for a relaxed evening, or I feel I have enough burdens of my own that I want her help with. Instead of being gentle and kind, I am critical and harsh. In my worse moments, I blame her for this. In my more self-aware moments, I'm very disappointed with myself.

Nor am I the Christian I want to be. It seems such a simple thing to know Christ through his word, reading the Bible daily and voraciously. It seems even more simple to prayerfully depend on the Lord moment by moment. So why is my Bible reading and prayer life so weak? It is even more simple to trust Christ, but I am reduced to fury and misery by the tiniest inconvenience.

In so many parts of my life, I am a disappointment to myself. But am I just being down on myself here? Is higher self-esteem or a more realistic understanding of the pressures I'm under the answer? No. I am a disappointment because I do not live up to the standards in the Bible. I should be disappointed because I have failed to live up to Christ's good, beautiful and objective standards. I am objectively disappointing. Most of the time, I should be far more disappointed with myself than I am.

If you are disappointed with yourself, then the first thing to recognise is that this is most likely a good thing—a blessing from God. That feeling is not the last word in our lives (or in this chapter). But it should be part of our story.

## THE ADULTEROUS KILLER AND THE END OF THE COVER-UP

David's world collapsed at the highpoint of his reign as king of Israel, at the most successful and secure time in his life. Until then, he had enjoyed a wonderfully close relationship with his Lord, and he was also the owner of a staggering promise from God: that his family line would continue eternally, because one of his descendants would rule for ever (2 Samuel 7 v 12-16).

Yet, despite all this, he comes to a point where looks at himself and says to his friend, Nathan the prophet:

I have sinned against the LORD. (2 Samuel 12 v 13)

And he is right. David has killed one of his friends, Uriah, a fellow-soldier and faithful member of David's bodyguard. On David's orders, Uriah has been left alone on a battlefield and butchered, simply to cover up the fact that David had had sex with Uriah's wife, Bathsheba, and had made her pregnant.

David is a miserable sinner, like me. He is also called a man after God's own heart (1 Samuel 13 v 14). How can this be? It is his capacity to see his sin and own it that makes David a man after God's own heart. He had the option to continue the cover-up. Nathan could have been silenced in the same way Uriah was. David could have made excuses. He could have pointed out his successes in other areas, as though the stench of his sin could be negated by the perfume of his partial obedience.

But he didn't do any of those things. David is able to see himself clearly, see what he has done, and see that he has sinned. David is deeply disappointed with himself, and he should be. But that disappointment drives him to God, rather than to despair. We are going to follow him.

## DISAPPOINTMENT

David expands on his admission of sin with the great song of repentance that is Psalm 51, the introduction to which says:

> A psalm of David. When the prophet Nathan came to
> him after David had committed adultery with Bathsheba.

David knows he needs great mercy from the Lord, because his sin is great and it is against the Lord. Read his words and think about how they compare with your own "sorrys" to God:

> I know my transgressions,
>     and my sin is always before me.
> Against you, you only, have I sinned
>     and done what is evil in your sight;
> so you are right in your verdict
>     and justified when you judge.
> Surely I was sinful at birth,

> sinful from the time my mother conceived me.
> Yet you desired faithfulness even in the womb;
> you taught me wisdom in that secret place.
>
> (Psalm 51 v 3-6)

When David insists that his sin is against God only, he is owning the full horror of what he has done. He has not only abused one of God's people and ended the earthly existence of another; he has abused God and attempted to live as though he did not exist. David pushes to the depths of his self-disappointment. If there is any voice within him suggesting he should make an excuse or belittle the seriousness of the sin, he does not listen to it.

David pushes down to the depths of his sin, and he pushes back to its origin. It is who he is. He was "sinful from the time my mother conceived me". He never had to learn to sin; it came to him naturally. It is the same with us. I am a sinner, by nature and behaviour. Just as an apple tree sprouts apples by its nature, so I sprout sin from my nature as a sinner. My situation is desperate.

To see this frees us from our knee-jerk reactions to our disappointment. Trying harder will not work—you're just a sinner trying harder. Learning more will not work—you're just a sinner with more knowledge. I'm not a flawed father because I lack effort or lack expertise. I am a disappointing dad because I am a sinner.

I am a sinning sinner who will face the judgment of God. Just because it is in my nature to sin that is no excuse. I still choose to sin, and I deserve to face God's wrath on my sin.

I don't know you, but I do know that you, like David and like me, are a sinner. And that should be the greatest source of self-disappointment to you. David did not hold back when he realised his sin. Peter wept bitterly over his (Luke 22 v 62). Paul viewed himself as the worst sinner he knew (1 Timothy 1 v 15).

And you. Are you self-disappointed enough?

## DELIVERANCE

David gets high marks for self-aware honesty. The problem is that all that is left when he sees himself rightly is despair. Unless... unless there is a God who stands ready to deliver him. And there is.

David knows that there is a road out of his disappointment. There is love and mercy in his Lord that is so great that it can make his dirty, sinful self as white as snow—whiter even:

> Cleanse me with hyssop, and I shall be clean;
> wash me, and I shall be whiter than snow.
> Let me hear joy and gladness;
> let the bones you have crushed rejoice.
> Hide your face from my sins
> and blot out all my iniquity.
> Create in me a pure heart, O God,
> and renew a steadfast spirit within me.
> Do not cast me from your presence
> or take your Holy Spirit from me.
> Restore to me the joy of your salvation
> and grant me a willing spirit, to sustain me.
>
> (Psalm 51 v 7-12)

Twigs from the hyssop plant were used to sprinkle blood in the sacrifices which God's people made at the tabernacle. And it was hyssop that was used to paint the doorframes of the houses of the Israelites with the blood of the lambs who had died, so that the destroying angel would pass over them as he judged Egypt (Exodus 12 v 22). David is asking for a sacrifice to take away his sins. He is asking to be painted with the blood of another who has borne his judgment. He is asking for God to do what David cannot—to make him clean.

David needed another Passover; he needed the cross of Christ. His own descendant would be the one whose blood would be shed in his place, for his sins, to make him clean.

To be disappointed with ourselves is a blessing, as it drives us to the depths of our sin, and to abandoning all hope in fixing our own problems. It is there that the cross of Christ stands as a tree of life. For on the cross, the core of who I am—a sinful heart—is gently prised from me, and I am given a new heart and a new spirit.

Who I am is different now. But that does not mean I am perfect, just as David was not. He had a new heart—a completely saved heart—but he still needed help with living with a pure heart—where his thoughts, words and actions aligned with his new life. David knows he is the Lord's. He also knows that there is a battle raging at the core of his very being. He has a new heart; but he still sins, he still lusts, he still murders. He has a new heart, and he needs a purified heart. He needs God's help to be who God has re-created him to be. So do you and I. We are perfect in God's sight, for our sins have been taken away and dealt with on the cross. We are imperfect in our lives, for we still sin. We will be perfect, but we are not yet perfect. It's the tension of the Christian life—I know I am Christ's, and I love that I'm Christ's, but I don't always live as though I'm Christ's. So, with David, we pray for the Lord to create a pure heart within us, even as we know he has, and he will.

Here is why self-disappointment need not drive you to despair—there is a cross that you can go to and have hope. There is an empty tomb that speaks of an eternal, perfect, sinless future. One day, you will be sinless; the old self, the sinful nature, the impure heart will be finally destroyed by the life of Christ in us. You will stand with Jesus and you will be pure, whiter than snow.

## PURPOSE RENEWED AND RESTORED

What is fascinating about Psalm 51 is that this new identity immediately gives David purpose. We would think that he had blown it. Even if he can be forgiven for such wickedness, surely he has lost his ministry? Surely he has disqualified himself from being king of God's people? Surely God will now replace him?

There are terrible consequences of David's sin, played out in his family through the rest of his life—but God does not remove him from his rule. Indeed, the restored David sees an even greater scope for his ministry:

> Then I will teach transgressors your ways,
>    so that sinners will turn back to you.
> Deliver me from the guilt of bloodshed, O God,
>    you who are God my Saviour,
>    and my tongue will sing of your righteousness.
> Open my lips, Lord,
>    and my mouth will declare your praise.
> You do not delight in sacrifice, or I would bring it;
>    you do not take pleasure in burnt offerings.
> My sacrifice, O God, is a broken spirit;
>    a broken and contrite heart
>    you, God, will not despise. (Psalm 51 v 13-17)

With a new and "broken" heart, David is well-suited to be used as an instrument in God's hands. This is a strange assertion. Surely the world needs to see strong, successful Christians, good, sorted people who show the power of God in their lives as they experience continual victory over sin and temptation? Not really. The world needs to see real Christians, who seek to obey their King out of love for him, who celebrate any progress but who are disappointed with their continual failures, and who sing not of their own goodness but of their God's mercy at the cross.

Your purpose in life is not to be perfect. Your purpose in life is to showcase God's grace to the imperfect. Imagine a mother caring for small children or a woman who has great management responsibilities at work. They are exhausted (maybe they are the same person, in which case she is doubly exhausted!). And sometimes they snap. They hurt those they should be caring for—kids or staff.

They could excuse it. They could ignore it. They could—should—be deeply disappointed by it.

But they need not despair about it. They can go to the cross. And then they can sing of the cross. They have an opportunity to apologise unreservedly to their children or their employees, to ask for forgiveness, to talk about the freedom of repentance. They can speak of being brokenhearted about their flaws and pure-hearted because of their Saviour.


## PERSPECTIVE

This purpose will not be in vain. It may feel weak, desperate and little. What can a sinner, or a struggling mum, or a snappy boss, hope to do for Christ? David thinks we can build God's kingdom:

> May it please you to prosper Zion,
>     to build up the walls of Jerusalem.
> Then you will delight in the sacrifices of the righteous,
>     in burnt offerings offered whole;
>         then bulls will be offered on your altar. (Psalm 51 v 18-19)

At first this seems to have nothing to do with the rest of the psalm! Why does he shift focus from his contrite heart to Zion's walls? The answer is simply that David is looking forward to the day when Christ returns. There will be an eternal city, a wonderful future for forgiven sinners like him and like us. David draws us into looking forward to Zion, to the eternal city bought for us by the blood of Christ and built up by the work of Christ.

Those who feel they need to be forgiven little love little, and will sing little. Those whose self-disappointment drives them to the cross will know they are forgiven much, and will love much and sing much. As we speak of God's mercy to us, and his offer of mercy to those around us who are disappointed with themselves but have no real idea why, we catch glimpses of the day when the earth will be filled with the knowledge of the glory of God, when Zion will prosper. The day is coming when Christ will come, and our disappointment will be ended.

## GOD DOES NOT NEED MORE THAN YOU CAN GIVE

Maybe, though, all this has left you more disappointed. You know you are a sinner, and you appreciate being a saved sinner. Your disappointment lies more in your lack of abilities, and you'd hoped this chapter would be about that. You wish you had a sharper mind to understand God's word better and remember it more. You wish you had more energy so you could get more done and serve more. You wish you were able to play the piano in church, or shift chairs before church, or bake cakes for after church... but you can't.

How disappointing. What a disappointment you are. If only you were someone else. Or rather, yourself, but better.

If this is you, then this is the bit of the chapter that aims to help you! First, make sure you're more disappointed with your sin against God than your service (or lack of it) for God.

And second, remember that God does not need more than you can give. And that God has given you just the abilities, energy and brain capacity that he wants you to have for the good of his people:

> There are different kinds of gifts, but the same Spirit distributes them. There are different kinds of service, but the same Lord ... in all of them and in everyone it is the same God at work ... he distributes them to each one, just as he determines. (1 Corinthians 12 v 4, 6, 11)

You do not have to desire the gifts that others have. Instead, you can be grateful that they have been given at all. And you do not need to worry that God wants you to do more than your mind, energy and abilities can manage. Instead, you can remember that God gave you just what he knows you need to do the good works he has written on your to-do list each day (Ephesians 2 v 10).

> Now if the foot should say, "Because I am not a hand, I do not belong to the body," it would not for that reason stop being part of the body. And if the ear should say, "Because I am not an eye, I do not belong to the body," it would not for that reason stop being part of the body. If the whole body were an eye, where would the sense of hearing be? If the whole body were an ear, where would the sense of smell be? But in fact God has placed the parts in the body, every one of them, just as he wanted them to be. If they were all one part, where would the body be? As it is, there are many parts, but one body.
>
> (1 Corinthians 12 v 15-20)

We can simply enjoy the gifts we have been given. The challenge comes when the gifts we have are not obviously seen during the organised life of the church. Everyone sees the preacher teaching the church on Sunday; very few see the mum teaching the children on Tuesday after school. Everyone sees the ministry to those struggling with addictions. Very few see the mercy shown over coffee to a friend with depression. Prayer warriors are easily identified in the monthly prayer meeting, but no one else sees the desperate rearguard actions of the spiritual war fought as tired saints bend over a photocopier, a changing mat, a pile of washing-up. Everyone sees the great work done by the Sunday school teachers, hard though it is. Very few see the hours of prayer put in weekly by the lady who taught Sunday school for forty-eight years, who is now housebound and yet still as concerned for children as when she was unpacking the miracles of Jesus for them.

The Lord sees. He cares. He is delighted. And he is never disappointed by someone who uses the gifts he has chosen to give them to love him and love others. Neither need you be.

If you want to do more than you have been given, then ask God by all means, and wait. He will surely bring people across your path whom you can love. He will give you gifts that will suit you, bless you and make you more like Christ. Just remember that Christ came as a servant, full of love, and that the ministry he delights in is that of a servant, full of love. This is our purpose: simple, glorious, Jesus-mirroring love. It can only be truly shown by the weak—by those with a broken, pure heart. Don't be disappointed by what you cannot do and who you cannot be. He isn't.

## LOOK IN THE MIRROR

Finish this chapter by considering your sin. Without excuse or explanation, think about who you are. You do not sin because you are tired. You do not sin because others treat you badly. You sin because you are a sinner. Can you see the desperation of your situation? Maybe you have some particular sin in mind. If so, then push down. That sin is merely the tip of the iceberg. Below the surface lurks a nature opposed to God. You are a rotten tree that should only produce rotten fruit. See yourself as you are. Most of us should be far more disappointed with ourselves than we are.

And then stop.

Put all that disappointment to one side and look at Christ on the cross. You were conceived a sinner, a rotten tree, but Christ has uprooted you and planted you beside streams of living water. He has taken your sin. Your sinful nature is no longer the real you. On his tree, as he died, your sin and your sinfulness died too.

Some of us need to stop making excuses. Others need to stop dwelling on our sin. Maybe you are utterly disappointed with yourself, and you feel that God must be so disappointed with you too. But, while God is grieved by your failures, you need to grasp that at the same time and in a deeper way your Father is not disappointed with you. He has taken away your sin and given you the beautiful, warm righteousness of Jesus. Your Father is not disappointed with you; he is as pleased with you as he is pleased with Jesus. And your Father will use you, in your brokenhearted new-heartedness, with the gifts he has chosen to give you, to love those he has placed in your path.

When you look at yourself, you should be disappointed. The face looking back from the mirror is that of a sinner. But the face looking back from the mirror is, in a very real sense, Christ. You are clothed in him. It is catching sight of both images in the mirror—the disappointing you and the glorious Christ in you—that enables you to admit your sin but not despair at your sin, and to sing of the mercy you enjoy. And it is understanding that the first image is fading and the second is eternal that makes us realise the magnitude of our Father's grace to us. We are disappointed with ourselves, and yet we sing with joy about it. How strange. How wonderful!

# 11. DISAPPOINTED WITH... GOD

I am really disappointed with God.

I am disappointed that it rained for the entire week when I was off work with my family. Glorious sunshine for the week before, and then it was more like January than June when we were on holiday. Couldn't God have simply reversed the order?

I'm disappointed that I lost my glasses on holiday. You could say I should have taken them off before splashing in the enormous waves, but God could have kept them on my nose, We try to be careful with money, and it is disappointing when God doesn't seem to help with that. God didn't come through.

More seriously, I am disappointed that God doesn't save more people and add them to our number. He did this daily in Acts, and yet we don't even see people saved monthly at our church. And I am disappointed about how sinful I still am. Change feels so painfully slow; I keep on being tempted in the same ways, falling into sin in the same ways, and repenting in the same ways. I don't understand why the Spirit doesn't work more quickly to make me like Jesus. God hasn't come through.

I am disappointed that God didn't save my friend from his

cancer. When I visited my friend in the hospital, and talked with the doctors, it was clear that he wouldn't live through the night. I prayed so hard for him, and in the morning I talked with him and his wife at his bedside. I am sure it was a miraculous answer to prayer, and then he died of the cancer a year later. There is great suffering and pain for his family still. There is also disappointment and confusion. It felt like God did come through, and then he didn't.

## GOD IS RESPONSIBLE FOR ALL YOUR DISAPPOINTMENTS

When you stop to think about it, if God is in control of the world, if Jesus is indeed King and Lord, then he is responsible for all our other disappointments. If I have a difficult marriage, isn't it because God didn't give my wife and I wisdom to choose suitable partners? Or that he didn't change us enough to help us live together? If my work is hard, couldn't Jesus give me another job, or deliver the promotion I have missed so often? If I have laboured to lead a children's group at church for years, seeing so many leave the church a year or two later, surely God could have done something?

If God is in control—and he is—then behind all your disappointments with your relationships, your circumstances, your ministry and yourself must lie disappointment with God. All those disappointments you've thought about as you read the previous four chapters—under all of them lay disappointment with him. God could have, should have, might have... and didn't. So often, in so many small and serious ways, it feels as if God doesn't come through.

But we can't say that! It must be wrong to feel disappointed with God. It must be arrogant for limited creatures to question the Ancient of Days, right? Who are we to question him?

Not only that, but it feels dangerous to feel disappointed with God. If God is disappointing, then surely all hope disappears, purpose is extinguished and perspective is overturned. If God turns out to be disappointing, what is the point? We simply don't want to pursue that thought; we push it aside. It's wrong, it's dangerous.

Not according to the Bible though.

The Bible does not push aside disappointment with God. Could it be that we retreat too quickly from dealing with this disappointment with God? Rather than simply telling us not to question, the Bible invites us to explore our disappointment with God, and emerge from the voyage with treasures of hope, purpose and perspective and even joy at how deeply satisfying the Lord is. When we taste and see, we will find that the Lord is indeed good. It is far more dangerous to hide disappointment with God than to confront it. Pushed down as a niggling doubt, it will grow and spread, and subtly obliterate our faith, joy and hope. We will become cynical, angry Christians—and very possibly, at some point, cynical, angry used-to-be-Christians. What we do with our disappointment in God matters.

## REALLY, WHAT IS THE POINT OF LIVING FOR GOD?

The power of facing up to disappointment in God, and finding surprising joy, was the discovery of Asaph, who wrote Psalms 50 and 73 – 83. One of the themes of his psalms is disappointment with the Lord. Psalm 73 is a good example. Asaph states his issue succinctly:

> Surely God is good to Israel,
> to those who are pure in heart.

> But as for me, my feet had almost slipped;
>
>> I had nearly lost my foothold.
>
> For I envied the arrogant
>
>> when I saw the prosperity of the wicked. (v 1-3)

Asaph's problem is the contrast between what he knows of God—that he is good—and what he experiences in his life: people he knows who are wicked and arrogant and ungodly, but who are doing very nicely without ever saying thank you very much. They are rich, healthy, popular and free from troubles. Yet they mock God: "How would God know? Does the Most High know anything?" (v 11).

Asaph envies these people. They seem to have it made, living a charmed life. Indeed, they seem to lead a blessed life. Has he got it wrong. Does God really care? What is the point of living for him?

> Surely in vain I have kept my heart pure
>
>> and have washed my hands in innocence.
>
> All day long I have been afflicted,
>
>> and every morning brings new punishments. (v 13-14)

Asaph has trusted God, and God hasn't come through for him. The wicked get the blessings, and he gets the punishments. He is disappointed with God.

We've got it wrong. We think that the danger is to feel disappointed with God. Psalm 73 tells us that we can feel disappointed with our Lord. The danger is that we stop in our disappointment with God. Too often we nurse a disappointment with God, but we are afraid to examine it too closely. If we have pledged our allegiance to Christ, we have a lot to lose if we find out that he is not the real thing. It feels less risky to duck the subject, and carry on. This is what we often do. But when we look at it like that, we realise it simply should not be an option. If Christ cannot satisfy the deepest desires of our hearts, then he is not the God he made himself out to be, and he is not worth following.

There is nothing reserved or polite about Psalm 73. Asaph isn't putting on a Sunday-morning, everything's-fine face. He is disappointed with God. And he is willing to confront that, and confront God with it. He acknowledges his disappointments, and he obviously feels them deeply. But crucially, he doesn't stay there, close to giving up. Instead, he picks himself up and heads for Jerusalem.

## INTO THE TEMPLE

Let's follow Asaph down the road to the sanctuary of God, to the temple:

> When I tried to understand all this,
>     it troubled me deeply
> till I entered the sanctuary of God;
>     then I understood their final destiny.
> Surely you place them on slippery ground;
>     you cast them down to ruin.
> How suddenly are they destroyed,
>     completely swept away by terrors!
> They are like a dream when one awakes;
>     when you arise, LORD,
>     you will despise them as fantasies. (v 16-20)

Here is the answer to the disappointments with God that this life, and the way he has designed this life, so easily provokes. What we see now is not the end of the story. The reality of judgment gives Asaph perspective. The blessings of the wicked rich are temporary. Their final destiny is not satisfaction, but ruin. Their sense of security, peace, importance and wealth is a fantasy that will be swept away in a moment.

Think about what Asaph saw when he "entered the sanctuary". Before him is the great curtain, speaking of the separation between the perfect God and sinful people, telling sinners that they cannot enter his presence because they cannot survive in the presence of holy perfection. But behind him is the altar, speaking of the truth that sacrifices can be made that forgive sin and remove the barrier between holiness and sin, Creator and creatures, telling sinners that there is a way to live with God. There, Asaph sees that there is judgment of wickedness, arrogance and mockery. And there is forgiveness for those who are covered by the blood of the sacrifices that God provides. The sanctuary tells Asaph that in judgment and in salvation, God comes through.

Asaph encounters God at the curtain and the altar. We encounter God at the cross:

> With a loud cry, Jesus breathed his last. The curtain of
> the temple was torn in two from top to bottom.
>
> (Mark 15 v 37-38)

We come into the sanctuary through the now-torn curtain and the blood of *the* sacrifice: the blood of Christ. We can come in because the one good Son of Man was punished so that we— wicked, arrogant and mocking as we have been—could be forgiven and blessed. When we feel disappointed with God, we need to head straight away to the sanctuary, to the cross where our sacrifice shed his blood. When we feel that God is not coming through for us, the cross says, *He already has.*

Standing at the cross, like Asaph standing in the sanctuary, we regain perspective. Rather than assessing God's performance in terms of the little things we see or don't see (and don't understand), we see the full picture laid out. We see eternity. We see that our past was one of sin and judgment, but that now, since the judgment of God has fallen on the Son of God, we are free. Our future—our eternal future—is one of utter satisfaction at the right hand of the kindest Father. The things we want, the things that make us feel God didn't come through, are important, yes; but they are also so small. He came through, he gave us Christ, and he will give us the cosmos.

And this is the amazing truth: that whatever else God has not chosen to give us, he has given us the best thing he has to give us: himself. So Asaph realises that...

> I am always with you;
>     you hold me by my right hand.
> You guide me with your counsel,
>     and afterwards you will take me into glory.
> Whom have I in heaven but you?
>     And earth has nothing I desire besides you.
> My flesh and my heart may fail,
>     but God is the strength of my heart
>     and my portion for ever.
> Those who are far from you will perish;
>     you destroy all who are unfaithful to you.
> But as for me, it is good to be near God.
>     I have made the Sovereign LORD my refuge;
>     I will tell of all your deeds. (Psalm 73 v 23-28)

How easy it is to assess God's goodness by the wrong criteria: Do we have a family? How close are we to our friends? How fulfilled are we by our work? How much of the world have we seen? But God has given us something greater than any of these, and we will always find him disappointing if we seek less than he gives us. We would be amazed at a girlfriend who ignored the perfect, glittering diamond shimmering in the golden circle that fits her finger perfectly, because she didn't quite like the colour of the box in which her boyfriend, down on one knee, presented it to her.

Asaph realised that he was disappointed in God because he was seeking the wrong things from God. It wasn't that he was expecting too much (as we sometimes fear must be the case). No, he was expecting too little from the Lord. God did not want to give him mere blessing. God gave himself to Asaph:

> Yet I am always with you;
>     you hold me by my right hand.
> You guide me with your counsel,
>     and afterward you will take me into glory. (v 23-24)

God holds Asaph, God guides him, and God will take him into glory. God has come through for him. God will keep coming through for him. It's just that Asaph has been looking in the wrong place.

## JOURNEYS AND DESTINATIONS

When I was young, we drove a long way on holiday each year. The journeys were exciting, full of the promise of sand, sea and ice cream. They were also somewhat tedious. The car would get hot and uncomfortable. My brother would be annoying (he said the same thing about me, but obviously my complaint was more justified). Sometimes we didn't get our favourite sweets to enjoy on the journey.

But that was all OK. The journey was not the holiday. It was just the way of getting to the holiday. However good the journey was, even if the car was cool, my brother was fine, and the sweets were supplied—it still wasn't the holiday. However bad the journey was—we were still on the way to the holiday. If the journey had been the holiday, that would have been terribly disappointing. But no one made that mistake. The journey was not the holiday.

And then we got there. When you catch the first glimpse of the sea, the whingeing from the back seat stops. When you feel the first wave slide over your feet, the miles between leaving and arriving seem far fewer than when you were in a tailback with everyone needing the toilet. By the time you are a couple of days into the holiday, you can even laugh about the arguments in the car.

I wonder if we sometimes forget that we are not on the holiday yet. I wonder if we sometimes forget where our good Father is taking us. We are on a journey to the promised land—and we are not there yet. We should not judge our Lord by the nature of the journey, without ever taking into account the destination. He has already paid the price for us to stay in the promised land. He is in the front seat, with us every mile of the journey.

One day we will get there. As the light, far richer than any sunrise, floods the new creation, maybe a friend will clap you on the back, shout, "Race you!" and sprint towards the crystal clear waters flowing from the throne. Maybe the disappointment will be sucked to nothing as you whoop and follow. Maybe you will slowly breathe out, feeling pain and frustration slip from you as the light of Christ washes over you. Maybe you won't even think of it as you realise the friend who slapped you on the back was the "Friend of sinners", and his smile as he beckons over his shoulder for you to follow fills your heart and mind so totally that there is no room for another thought, good or bad.

Like Asaph, we need to remember where we are going. We do this by going into the sanctuary, by going to the cross of Christ and remembering what he has bought for us. We are heading for the new creation, and Jesus is with us, taking us by the hand and making sure we don't miss the path. It is a hard path—he warned us it would be—but it is the route, not the destination.

## THE FATHER'S DOOR IS OPEN (WELL, TORN, ACTUALLY)

We do not need to fear expressing our disappointment. We will see more of this in the next chapter, but for now we need to see that the church is the safe and glorious place where we see God. The church is the family in the car; we are on our way together to the new creation. It is a safe place in which to complain that your brother has eaten all the purple sweets. It is fine to ask, "Are we there yet?" We can bring our disappointment, even with God, to our brothers and sisters, without fear. We will not upset the faith of others, because God has given himself to us. He has given us such a great gift that we can never find him disappointing when we see him rightly. To see him rightly we need to see him together. We need each other to see and know the Lord who died for us.

There is a depth of joy in being with God that cannot be found anywhere else. We see it reflected in the contentment of a little child with their mother or father. Sylvia, my littlest girl, occasionally pushes my study door to see if it is open. I hear her shout of triumph when it is, and she totters through with her arms stretched out to me. She just enjoys being with me for a bit. She is happy to be with her father. Her father is happy to be with her, and still more happy that she is happy to be with him. And if that is an incentive to me to forget to close my study door much of the time, how much more does our perfect Father keep open the door to his throne room? We know the answer to that—his door was a curtain, and he ripped it in two. He came through for you so that you can come through to him.

So, however you are disappointed right now, acknowledge that wrapped up in that disappointment is a disappointment that God didn't come through. You are allowed to feel this way. Voice your disappointment with him. I have seen the sadness and loss that an unspoken, unexamined disappointment with Jesus has brought into the lives of brothers and sisters I love. Stand on that disappointment in order to get a better view of the cross. There, we see that God came through for us. There, you encounter the simple reality, along with Asaph, that "it is good to be near God". Whatever else you do not have and wish you did, you have him. And one day, with him, you will have everything. Except a feeling of disappointment.

# 12. LOCK SHIELDS AND STAND FIRM

When I was planning this book, I outlined my hopes for your response to each chapter. This is an extremely useful exercise, but when I read again my hope for this chapter, it frightened me. It seems too much to ask:

> *Within the first five minutes of his next small-group meeting, the reader will say that the group must address the issue of disappointment, and vulnerably open up their own struggles and invite the group to speak the gospel into them.*

How do you react to that? When I think of this sort of vulnerability with others, I am both attracted and terrified. I love the idea of being known and having brothers and sisters in Christ speak into my life at the deepest points; and I am alarmed at the idea of being known, and of what they might say and think. It is a dangerous thing to get out your hopes and fears and entrust them to others.

But it is what church is for. Christ has called us together into his church to stand together against our enemies, and those enemies include over-disappointment and under-disappointment. We are known by God, and we are one with him and his people. It makes sense to be known by them too. It makes deep, gospel sense.

## THE TESTUDO CHURCH

We see why we need to, and how we can, stick together, as Paul draws to the end of his letter to the church in Ephesus:

> Finally, be strong in the Lord and in his mighty power. Put on the full armour of God, so that you can take your stand against the devil's schemes. For our struggle is not against flesh and blood, but against the rulers, against the authorities, against the powers of this dark world and against the spiritual forces of evil in the heavenly realms. (Ephesians 6 v 10-12)

One of the devil's schemes is to use our disappointment to draw us away from Christ rather than push us towards him. He does this by making us keep quiet about it. If I am disappointed in my marriage, but never talk about it with anyone, he can use that to strangle my joy and sow bitterness, which will grow into lovelessness and maybe even an affair. If I am disappointed by my lack of marriage, but never talk about it with anyone, that is ground he will use to grow a sense of entitlement, which flowers into sexual immorality or marrying disobediently. While those seeds that bloom in sin begin to grow, he makes sure they are not rooted out by telling me that it is impossible for me to talk with friends at church about, for example, disappointment in my marriage. "After all," he whispers, "it is hardly fair on your wife to tell people if you are finding marriage disappointing at the moment." Or, "You are hardly going to look godly if you open up to your struggles with your singleness. Anyway, everyone else has issues too. Plus, they can't help, can they? Just keep quiet."

The problem is that when he cuts us off from our brothers and sisters, the devil knows that we have little chance against him. We are not meant to take him on in single combat—Christ has already won that battle for us. As so often in the New Testament, the "yous" in Ephesians 6 are plural, not singular. It is written to a church, not a Christian. This is "our struggle", not "my struggle". We are meant to stand firm together, with our shields locked. The picture in verses 13-17—of putting on "the full armour of God, so that when the day of evil comes, you may be able to stand your ground, and after you have done everything, to stand"—is not of a warrior getting ready for battle, but of a squad, a Roman unit.

The armour Paul details is Roman armour, and the Romans had conquered half the known world by fighting together against those who fought as a group of individuals. Roman legionaries sometimes fought in *testudo* (tortoise) formation. The unit would form into a block of men, with those at the front, rear and sides overlapping their shields outwards, and the soldiers in the middle holding theirs above their heads. No soldier was entirely defended by his own shield, but each was defended from all directions by the overlapping shields of his comrades. Formed like this, the unit was virtually impenetrable.

This is the church. The way we stand our ground against the schemes of the devil is to do so together. We keep truth firmly buckled on by speaking it to each other. Our hearts are protected by the righteousness of Christ, and we see and hear that righteousness in our church family. We storm into the breach together to take the gospel of peace to the nations, and as we do so, our shields are held up—it is our faith together that forms the shield wall to protect the church. If my shield is down, then I'm in danger, and so you raise yours to catch the arrow. Next week, I'll do the same for you.

When it comes to disappointment, I am sure that a huge problem is that we do not fight its dangers together. We need to tease out where in our lives we should be disappointed, but are not. We need to see where our disappointment is simply wrong, and where our disappointment is legitimate but has grown too large. We need to let the gospel of Jesus Christ affect the way we feel. These are incredibly hard things to do for ourselves. I'd suggest they are impossible for you to achieve. But you are not meant to. We need to fight for joy in a disappointing world together.

## THE DEEP PROBLEM OF BEING FINE, THANKS

We are all tempted to put on a good front to the world. There are obviously times when this is appropriate. When a colleague asks you how you are on a Monday morning, it is not the time or place to go into the details of your struggles with singleness or your impatience with the kids over the last month.

What about when a church member asks you the same question as you chat together after the church service on a Sunday morning?

We are so tempted to keep our front up. Instead of gospel armour, we wear "fine, thanks" armour. The entire church is usually "fine":

"Hi, John, how are you doing?"

"Fine, thanks. [Apart from my increasing outbursts of anger at work] You?"

"Fine. [Apart from the row we had on the way to church, which repeats itself week after week. I didn't want to be this guy]. How was your holiday?"

"Yeah, it was good. [Apart from the weather, the lack of sleep, and losing my glasses in the sea] Anyway, did you see the game yesterday?"

This is fine—except for the fact that we are not fine.

I find it so tiring. I try to give the impression that I've got it all together, that my life is always sunny. It is hard work pretending, trying to kid myself and others that I am not disappointed. It is useless for my friends as well, because it means they cannot admit to their struggles and frustrations, as they assume that we're all meant to be "fine" and that they are letting the side down to say otherwise. And it undermines our witness to our community too. When a brokenhearted, desperately disappointed friend comes to church with me, he will know that Jesus is not interested in him because he is a mess, and he could never fit in with these sorted Christians in my church who are all fine. When we refuse to open up, we preach that "The Son of Man came to seek and save the fine, the sorted and the smiling".

Yes, maybe Sunday morning after church is not the time to open up completely. But it is also not the time to hide behind "fine". Are we willing to be known, in all our disappointed truthfulness, and wiling to listen to others as they open up to us? Maybe on Sunday the answer should be, "I've got a few things going on, not quite fine, but can we talk later?". Then maybe that later talk can be real, open, and trusting that your brother has his shield out to protect you.

We need to talk about our disappointments. When we do does not matter, but that we do so is essential.

## KNOWN TRULY BY ALL AND FULLY BY SOME

We need to speak the truth about ourselves and our struggles. We then need to speak gospel truth to others in their struggles (and to hear it spoken by them into ours). We need to be "speaking the truth in love" so that we "grow to become in every respect the mature body of him who is the head, that is, Christ" (Ephesians 4 v 15). You (plural and singular) will never grow to become more like Jesus if you are not willing to speak truth lovingly about yourself and to others.

So will you (singular) make a start? What disappointments are you facing in your life? Who could you talk them through with? If you are a member of a small group, find a disappointment to bring up next time, with the expectation that hope and wisdom will be poured into your frustration. Work is a good one—in some ways it's much easier for you and the group to engage with than family, marriage or other more intimate disappointments. But don't stop there—after all, the other disappointments are often more significant. As the culture of your group grows to understand and engage with the meaninglessness of life under the sun, who knows how Christ might use it to open and transform your lives?

This is going to be hard and require love. It is hard to lay yourself open before others. Sometimes it is wise to hold back, not for your sake but for others—it will be hard for the unemployed member of your group to hear of your disappointment with your £5,000 bonus, and when our disappointments involve people others know, we need to be careful about when and where we speak, and make sure we speak positively as well as honestly (this is why often pastors are the least known people in the church—we never open up for fear of sounding critical or encouraging gossip).

So how do we move to a place where we are able to bring

out our disappointments and draw our church family into speaking the gospel together into one another's hearts?

The first thing we need to do is to speak honestly to ourselves. If we have suppressed the disappointment, bottling it up and avoiding facing it, then we are not going to share it. But knowing that we can share it, and expecting to find love and grace when we do, can help us to see that it is there in the first place. We need to own that we are disappointed rather than keeping on chasing the wind. One of the goals of Ecclesiastes is to drum into us that much of what our world sees as achievement is simply energetic pointlessness.

Next, speak honestly to God, as Asaph did.

Then, once you see your disappointment, you can speak to your church. I'm not suggesting an announcement from the front to the whole gathering! Church is a family, and being open in a large family does not mean full disclosure to everyone; it means openness within relationship. So everyone in my church should know me truly, and some should know me fully. I am well aware that I fall short. It is worth aiming at, though, and I will keep doing so.

Being known truly means that as people get to know you better, they should not feel surprised. They should not find a "real" you behind the persona. They should find consistency. In your working life, you often need to act professionally, which means presenting your professional side (I want a doctor to calmly, thoughtfully deal with my illness, not hear from her how her marriage is going!). But in church, no one is a professional. We are brothers and sisters. Be real.

Being known fully means that some members of your church family will be allowed to see, and speak into, the depths of who you are, because you've opened yourself to them. That is how a family works.

Imagine a large family, with adult children. They all spend time together, gathering for special occasions. When one brother is in trouble, the other siblings rally round to help. There are always plenty of hands to pack a van when someone needs to move house, and plenty of help when a baby comes. Mark and Tim are particularly close though, and play computer games together one night a week. Over the evening they talk about everything—work, marriage, family, God. When Mark hits a difficult patch in his marriage, it is natural that he talks to Tim about it. He also goes to his mum and dad to seek wisdom, as they have a good marriage. He might turn to Sally as well, his sister, as she works as a counsellor and will have some wisdom.

But at the same time, he probably won't bring the issues up round the Christmas table as the whole family gathers (or most of the family—this is a real family, so they too experience the diplomatic quagmire of who goes where for Christmas). But if someone asks him how he's doing, he'll try to be honest. If the issue is serious enough, and doesn't involve betraying or criticising someone else, then he'll pour it all out to the first brother or sister he sees. Family is safe.

Church family should be the same. Some disappointments are shareable with anyone and everyone. Some sadnesses are shareable with some, but not all. Some struggles—perhaps especially those that involve other people—are shareable with only one or two. And, depending on your character, it may even be that you need to give others time and space to share their lives with you rather than plunging in straight away with the problems and tensions in yours. But for most of us, the trouble is not us sharing too much, too often, but sharing nothing at all, ever.

So here are three things I would love you to do with your church. None are easy. All are liberating. It is how we lock shields:

First, be honest in response to questions. Find some better answers to the question of how we're doing than "Fine thanks". How about, "Thanks for asking. Not so well, but now's not the time, really. I'm chatting it through with David and Sean—please pray that they'd speak the gospel to me and that I'd listen to it." Or, "There's an issue in our family. I can't go into it, but could you pray for wisdom for me." Or, "Not great. Would you have time for a drink this week? I need someone to speak truth to me." Be truly known by all.

Second, be fully known by some. Generally speaking, my "community group" at church know me more fully than some others. Some within that group, and others outside it, know me as fully as anyone apart from my wife. I still often wear my "fine, thanks" mask, and am learning to take it off more and more. But God has gifted me with good brothers and sisters, and it is immensely joyful to be able to get out my disappointments in a Friday morning prayer meeting with three wise and godly brothers who are willing, when necessary, to cut them (and me) down to size. I need their wisdom, their speaking of the Scripture and their prayer. My joy in Christ often comes through them.

You need this. And others in your church do, too. Yes, many of us lead busy lives, but if we are trying to live Christian lives, we'll find the time. Who can you be fully known by? How will you make this possible?

Third, when you are struggling with disappointment, be willing to talk about it with the first brother or sister you see, in a way that is appropriate within the reality of that relationship and fair to anyone else involved in the reason for that struggle. I remember once meeting up with a much older, wiser Christian than me for a particular purpose, when he asked me to speak the gospel into his life about a completely different area. He trusted me to do so because of his trust in the Spirit and despite the fact that he was a far more mature believer than me. You don't need an expert to speak the gospel to you. You need a believer.

I've found that the Lord often puts just the right person across my path, even if often it is not someone I would have guessed at. It is risky to entrust yourself to a brother or sister when you are not sure how they will respond. It is not easy, but I have found that taking a risk in love and faith is a blessing in itself.

It is so refreshing to be real. It is so encouraging to others that they can be real. And it is compelling to those around us. In our dealings with our neighbours and colleagues, it can be easy to hide behind the mask when it would be ok to lower it. When we are known in church, helped by others, we can be known in the world. We can share the help and change that Christ brings. We can show how the power of disappointment has been broken by the cross of Christ and how it is possible to live with real disappointment and deep joy at the same time. That is an attractive gospel in our wealthy, successful and yet strangely dissatisfied day.

## WHAT DO I SAY?

So a brother or sister opens up to you about disappointments (maybe they've been reading this chapter too, and decided to see what happens if they put it into practice). *What do you say?!* The simple answer is to talk about Christ's return—to put our faith in our King who is coming. If our faith is only about this life, it has no power, and we are to be pitied (1 Corinthians 15 v 19). We need to recapture faith in the Christ who is coming. Once we see the future rightly, we can see that disappointment is not our destiny. This gives us the confidence to allow disappointment out into the open and look at it more closely.

We do this by being honest about our own disappointments, creating a culture where these things can be said. We respond to others opening up by admitting where we empathise with their disappointment. But we don't stop there. We do not have to resort to our own wisdom or to worldly platitudes when we have the gospel of Jesus Christ. We can speak liberating truth into the disappointments our friends are struggling with.

One way to do this is to bear in mind the hope, purpose and perspective that chapters 4 to 6 outlined. In the context of a thankfulness that magnifies Jesus, these are weapons to use in our fights against the enemy when he wields disappointment as a weapon against our faith.

Perhaps your friend is finding work disappointing. You can help her to see that this is, at least in part, a right disappointment. She should expect work in this world to be a blessing from God, but also a toilsome chore. It is a good thing that is tarnished by sin, so it will be disappointing.

Then you can show how the coming return of Christ gives her hope. Unfulfilling work is not her destiny. She is destined to serve Christ and his new creation in ways that are deeply satisfying. The same return will help her to keep perspective on her work. It is not meaningless, however disappointing it is. It is a context in which she can work as one serving Christ now. You can ask yourself whether you can help her to work through what that might look like in the gritty specifics of her particular work with its particular disappointments. As well as a new perspective, you could also talk about the new purpose she has. Are there opportunities at work to love well? Whether it is noticed or not by her colleagues or customers, it will be noticed by her King.

This is not about pulling out a "hope, purpose, perspective" mantra that will cause your friends to roll their eyes and revert to "Fine thanks" when they see you. It's about loving and listening, and then speaking carefully and kindly, but also pointing to gospel truths clearly. This is risky—people do not always particularly want to hear it, and often transformation is not instantaneous. But there is huge power in these gospel ideas to impact every disappointment we face.

## WILL YOU DO IT?

This may be a long war. Disappointment is not a season, but a lifetime. While suffering may be a nuclear bomb that the devil detonates in our lives in an attempt to cause us to put down our guard and run from the Christian life, disappointment is his stealth weapon that he deploy in a war of attrition, aiming to push us slowly, imperceptibly, off the battlefield. It is impossible to stand alone. But you do not have to. You have a Commander who has won the battle for you. And you have a *testudo* who stand firm with you. They can fight for you as you let them. They need you to fight for them as they let you. Speak the truth in love to one another, and listen to the truth in love from one another, and you will stand firm, and stand joyful.

So the aim was that within the first five minutes of your next small-group meeting, you will say that the group must address the issue of disappointment, and vulnerably open up your struggles and invite the group to speak the gospel into them.

This still terrifies me, and may well terrify you. But don't you love this level of togetherness in the fight for joyful faithfulness? Don't you want to take the risk and open up, and find the joy of standing firm with others, just as the Lord intended? Don't you want to get beyond superficiality and suppressed disappointment? What might the Lord do for you and your brothers and sisters if you do this? I am praying for you, that this might happen.

# 13. BUT GOD

> Praise be to the God and Father of our Lord Jesus Christ!
> In his great mercy he has given us new birth into a living
> hope through the resurrection of Jesus Christ from the
> dead, and into an inheritance that can never perish,
> spoil or fade. This inheritance is kept in heaven for you,
> who through faith are shielded by God's power until the
> coming of the salvation that is ready to be revealed in
> the last time. In all this you greatly rejoice, though now
> for a little while you may have had to suffer grief in all
> kinds of trials. (1 Peter 1 v 3-6)

These are words worth memorising, because one day you will
see what they describe with your eyes. One day you will stand
in your inheritance—one that can never end, which will never
be contaminated by sin, and whose pleasures will never grow
boring, dull or repetitive.

That is not your world right now. You live in a world of
trials, and disappointment is the world's response to trials.
I do not know what tears of frustration you have cried over
the past day, week or year. I suspect there will have been the
bitter tears over what you did in sin, over the disappointments

you brought on yourself. There will also be the terrible tears of a friendship, a love even, betrayed. There will be the sighs at the small disappointments of life: the holidays that didn't live up to their promise, the unkindness of colleagues, the forgetfulness of friends.

There will be the wondering sadness over the paths you didn't take, the experiences you never had, the opportunities you turned down, the tantalising tyranny of "what if...?"

You know disappointment, and you will go on knowing disappointment. It lives with us all. It has the capacity to dominate us all. The question is not: Will you be disappointed? The question is: How will you deal with your disappointment?

Here is how. Remember that your disappointment will end. It will be swept away by the coming of the risen Christ. God himself will come and live with us. There is no disappointment in him—he is always more than we could even imagine. There is joy in him—more than we could even dream.

God will not send you a message to cheer you up. He will not merely remove your memory of disappointment. He will come to you, and he will use his hand—his divine and wounded hand—to stroke the tears from your battle-smeared face. He will redeem your disappointments. He will, in ways we cannot dream of, bring joyful abundance where we sowed bitterness and frustration. He will sing the song of the sower and of the harvester, and he will rejoice over you with singing. He will catch you up in his arms and his salvation, and you will stand strong and tall, with Christ's arm on your shoulders as he leads in all those from all the nations who looked at the cross and saw his sacrifice for them, as all evil and death dies.

You will look to one side and see Solomon, with such deep joy in his eyes as Ecclesiastes is finally finished. You will glance to the other and see Asaph, with his feet firmly planted on the rock of the gospel and singing wholeheartedly of God's goodness.

Even if you are bitter and feel your life is meaningless as a result of the disappointment you experience, imagine the day when you stand in the place where there is no disappointment. I know you can't imagine it, but I think that trying to can make you smile. Call your disappointments to mind, parade them before you, and then imagine as best you can Christ standing before you. Do you think you will even notice those disappointments in the presence of his smile? In the gentle strength of his embrace? Try to think of the most amazing way he could strip away, redeem, answer and end each one of your disappointments. He will do better than you can imagine. Christ is coming for you.

What is the alternative? Maybe you can ignore your disappointment, though that is exhausting. Maybe you can wrap yourself in cynical indifference, though that is dehumanising. Perhaps you can rage against the world, though you will find yourself despairing. The cost of avoiding disappointment is avoiding life, and never understanding Jesus. He lived a life of burning disappointment: rejected, betrayed, killed. Jesus calls his followers to carry their crosses as he carried his, and that includes carrying the burden of disappointment. But not for ever. Not for long.

The world often promises us that we won't be disappointed. It is never totally true. Everything has its time. The joy fades after a while. Our failures spoil our successes. And everything perishes, rendering it pointless. There is no friend who is always true. There is no spouse who will love you perfectly.

There is no sinless child. There is no satisfying work. It is not true that you won't be disappointed. If this world is all there is, everything must be tinged with disappointment.

But you were not made for this world. You have an inheritance beyond it. And the One who promises that you will not be disappointed is the One who rose from the dead to triumph over every disappointment, and to overcome everything that fades and spoils and perishes. One day, you will find yourself totally satisfied; every desire far exceeded; every hope against hope met and met. Jesus will be this, all this and more than I know or imagine. There is no one like him, and you will be with him, you will be his, you will live. You will not be disappointed.

Disappointment, left unchecked, tends to dominate. It tends to put a "but..." at the end of every good thing.

The Bible reverses the "but..." It shows me that very often I should be more disappointed, not less. It shows me that I am more sinful than I would like to admit. That the world is more frustrating that I care to think. That what we chase is more pointless than I can bear to acknowledge.

Your life is disappointing. How it turned out is disappointing. Most of all, you are disappointing. Yet if you are following Jesus, none of that is the last word. Yes, there are real, painful, ongoing disappointments...

But God has taken you as his.

But God has sent his Son for you, to die for you, to win you, to bring you back to him.

But God has forgiven your sin.

But God has redeemed, used and transformed your disappointment.

But God has given you a new heart, a new hope, a new success, a new future.

But God has given you an inheritance that will never spoil, perish or fade.

But the One who you will stand before at the judgment is the One who hung on the cross to save you.

But God will send his Son again to wipe away your tears and give you your heart's desires.

But God has given you himself.

But *God*.

# LIVEDIFFERENT

## LIVING WITHOUT WORRY

If you ever worry, and would love to worry less, this book is for you. You will not find trite, easy answers; but you will find real ones, as you discover what worry is, why you feel it, and how you can replace it with an experience of real, lasting peace in all the ups and downs of your life.

*An accessible must-read for anyone who wants to begin the journey of worrying less.*

**HELEN THORNE, TRAINING MANAGER AT LONDON CITY MISSION**

## HONEST EVANGELISM

*How to talk about Jesus even when it's tough*

Rico Tice

## YOU CAN REALLY GROW

*How to thrive in your Christian life*

John Hindley

## SERVING WITHOUT SINKING

*How to serve Christ and keep your joy*

John Hindley

# thegoodbook
## COMPANY

*Opening up the Bible*

At The Good Book Company, we are dedicated to helping Christians and local churches grow. We believe that God's growth process always starts with hearing clearly what he has said to us through his timeless word—the Bible.

Ever since we opened our doors in 1991, we have been striving to produce resources that honour God in the way the Bible is used. We have grown to become an international provider of user-friendly resources to the Christian community, with believers of all backgrounds and denominations using our Bible studies, books, evangelistic resources, DVD-based courses and training events.

We want to equip ordinary Christians to live for Christ day by day, and churches to grow in their knowledge of God, their love for one another, and the effectiveness of their outreach.

Call us for a discussion of your needs or visit one of our local websites for more information on the resources and services we provide.

Your friends at The Good Book Company

---

**UK & EUROPE**       thegoodbook.co.uk       0333 123 0880
**NORTH AMERICA**    thegoodbook.com    866 244 2165
**AUSTRALIA**    thegoodbook.com.au    (02) 6100 4211
**NEW ZEALAND**    thegoodbook.co.nz    (+64) 3 343 2463

 **WWW.CHRISTIANITYEXPLORED.ORG**
Our partner site is a great place for those exploring the Christian faith, with a clear explanation of the good news, powerful testimonies and answers to difficult questions.